HEALING CHILDHOOD TRAUMA 2-1 SERIES

NANCY LOYAT

CONTENTS

EPIGRAPH

When I began this book in 2022, I didn't realize I was using DBT and CBT techniques as part of my healing process, precisely the grounding technique and journaling triggers. I put into practice what I learned in the group sessions I attended. I mainly focused on the grounding technique practice since it helped me with short-term issues. I am aware that this can be tedious at the very beginning. I encourage you to try my prepared challenge to measure your progress. This tool has opened up so many new horizons for me that I couldn't not share it with others like me who have suffered because of their inability to speak and feel what they feel.

In Chapter 7, you will find the link (or QR code for the print version) to download the short document. Understanding and expressing our needs is a skill that can be developed.

May this begin a new era for you, one in which you can identify dissociation (or emotional numbness) and start feeling and naming your needs.

Introduction

Children are the most trusting, innocent beings. Before they grow and adapt to the harsh world, they are open to everyone and everything; they are truthful, lively, and see the best in people, especially those close to them.

Imagine if one of the most heinous actions were committed against such a child, by adults he trusted or his parents trusted.

When done to an adult, it is heartbreaking. When done to a child, it breaks a lot more than just the heart.

It can break one's psyche for years, or even decades. It can shatter the memories of the cells that make up that child's body, and the cells will hold that destructive energy all throughout adulthood.

This is what happens when someone is forced to undergo childhood sexual abuse.

The odds of this crime occurring, without justice, is so hopelessly bleak that it boggles the mind. It can happen under anyone's nose. Even more, the aftereffects of this act can also occur to someone under everyone's nose, and no one would be able to tell. Inexplicable depression, anxiety, and self-destructive behaviors; they could plague you and no one, not even you, can understand why.

If you have experienced childhood sexual abuse, you know that it can follow you like a dreadful black dog. No matter how far you run, its shadow remains a few steps behind you. No matter how much you try to forget, the memories resurface every once a while -- or more often -- against your will. No matter how much you try to move on with your life and heal, the fact that this happened to you as a child falls heavy on your shoulders, pinning you down, shackling you.

I didn't remember the facts of my abuse before I reached the age of 31 years old. For the first 30 years of my life, I had no idea why I was overreacting to simple situations. That inexplicably made this part of myself even harder to withstand. I had a deep rage inside, but there was not a clear, external cause that I could attribute this to. Only when the memories came back to me did I realize that the anger was a remnant of the abuse, buried within my psyche. Not only that, but I also perceived hatred or anger from others on instinct, without any rational reason. That too, I realized, was just my perception of other people. I was wired to expect people to negatively react towards me, for as long as I apprehended it. I was always waiting for an argument or conflict to explode.

At this point, all you want is to free yourself, to stop being just a victim and a survivor, and to finally empower yourself to thrive. Maybe you've been to therapy or counseling, and no matter how hard you try, you can't seem to consistently put what you learned into practice. You want to deal with your emotions, to manage them when you get upset or triggered easily when you do self-sabotage behaviors like running away from responsibility or avoiding the social life you've always wanted. You would like a break from being wracked with misaimed guilt. You want to figure out how to take positive action, despite all your strong emotions. You want to create and maintain healthy relationships, in which you are miraculously able to identify and vocalize your needs. You'd like to improve your life with your significant other, with your work or career, and with your family. Most importantly, you want to know more about yourself and what is going on in your mind, to give yourself the peace and justice you deserve.

These desires are ones that every human on this earth wants.

However, these are all the more challenging to you than they are to others. The dreadful grip of childhood sexual abuse -- and all its associated symptoms -- is holding you back in your present life.

I know because I've been there.

As someone with a history of childhood sexual abuse, I have dealt with the aftereffects for years on end. For many, it happens similarly to my experience: there is a blockage in the mind when it comes to certain childhood memories. You can vaguely remember some things, but it feels surreal, like a nightmare or a figment of your wild imagination. Some may not have any memories of the event(s) at all. Then, you go through your adolescent and adult years dealing with a myriad of mysterious problems.

Mental health issues, depression, generalized anxiety, panic attacks, eating disorders... for me, it was dissociation. I was intimately familiar with what dissociation felt like long before I knew what it was and before I realized it wasn't normal. All I knew is that sometimes when triggered by certain stimuli, be it a word, media, a film, an object, a smell, or stress, I would simply disconnect from reality. Every time it happened, it was practically the same: it felt almost like an out-of-body experience. I don't hear anymore and I am under the influence of an emotion without being able to identify it. When I describe it to people, they often mention that it sounds like a wacky drug trip. They don't understand the worst parts of dissociation. When you are in that floaty, disembodied state, you suddenly lose sight or understanding of your sense of self, of your identity. Did you ever know who you are? Are you supposed to be here? Is that your body? Why are you here? Is your life even real? Do you exist? These feelings all wash over you like a wave, all at once, a series of panicked paranoid thoughts at the back of your mind, while you remain in this weird, suspended state. All you want then is to run away. Unconsciously, you disassociate.

Dissociation is then when you are living in the midst of life, and suddenly you are mentally pulled out of the present situation. Say you are in a conversation, and you are promptly thinking about something else, without conscious awareness of yourself doing this. The person talking to you sounds like a voice coming from the other side of a glass. Instead of participating in the conversation, you are observing things. Something catches your attention and you may interrupt the conversation to start talking about it. You are not in touch with the mood of the group or the setting. You are just reacting to things around you. Unfortunately, this isn't so good for maintaining relationships in the long run. Others may understandably perceive this as you ignoring them or not caring about what they are saying. However, you aren't purposefully trying to ignore them. Rather, you are unable to connect with something within you, with the darker parts of yourself. Guilt or shame is always at the back of your mind, stopping you from being truly present. Any word, object, or place can trigger this dissociative behavior. If you are not equipped to face it or understand it, then you are in bad shape.

I was in bad shape.

At times, when I came back to myself, I found that I had memory loss. My body would still remain functioning, sometimes automatically, during dissociation, and I might not remember what I did, said, or was about to do. Other times, I had anxiety attacks right afterward that jarred me and prevented me from going on with my day as planned. Worst of all is when I would be dragged into flashbacks of unpleasant memories from my younger years. Imagine getting ready for a meeting with your supervisor and suddenly you are reliving a horrifying childhood memory, the moment that changed everything. Sometimes, my body would react to something and I wouldn't know why. For instance, I would experience mysterious pain in my lower abdomen for no reason, with no underlying medical condition.

It was debilitating. Not only was it a shock to my system, mentally and physically, but it created so many issues in my work life. Trying to maintain and progress in a career is hard when you're forgetting things or having inconvenient symptoms at the wrong times.

Dissociation was a major part of most of my life. Yet I still had no idea what was going on inside me. The act of dissociating was like a wall between me and my inner child, who had been in deep, unseen pain for so long. I couldn't help her, because I couldn't see her.

So I ambled through life, trying to fit into my adult self and pretend there was nothing wrong. I pretended my difficulties at work could be solved by pushing up my sleeves and white-knuckling my way to success, like everyone else. Most of the time, this didn't work. I didn't have the skills that other functional people had and feeling inadequate, I would just give up and quit my job.

At a point in my life, an opportunity dropped right into my lap. It was one that had always been accessible to me, but I'd never had the courage or inspiration to try it out: attending a support group. I found a group tailored specifically for women who had been sexually abused in childhood. To this day, I still remember walking into that small room, filled with several chairs on which fellow victims, and survivors, sat waiting for the session to begin. I was wracked with nerves, but I felt a deep connection to the women there, because our shared experience felt so tangible, even before the support group leader started the session.

That support group changed my life. It made my inner child feel seen, heard, and valued. It uncovered answers to my issues in various areas of my life, be it work or relationships. It allowed me to tackle my dissociation head-on. And it is that support group, made up of some of the strongest, most admirable women I've ever met, that inspired me to write this book.

What my time in that support group has allowed me to do, I want to share, so that you too can:

    1. Take control of your life

2. Choose situations instead of letting them happen to you

3. Nurture respect for yourself and others

4. Ask directly what you want for yourself

5. Release negative energy

6. Achieve personal autonomy

7. Respond, rather than react

8. Know your needs

In this book, I will discuss what I have learned from my experience with childhood sexual abuse and its effects: dissociation, depression, anxiety, or feeling stuck in the memories. I am not a counselor, therapist, or psychologist, but the insights I have gotten from research, as well as my personal life, can help you break out of the mental chains of your past, learn to meet your own needs, and *finally* address the emotions locked in your body from a young age, that you must validate, accept, and manage.

Once you can release those stuck emotions, you are free to promote a new perspective on your life. With the strategies in this book, as well as a quick 3-step solution to overcome anxiety, you can better regulate yourself in the midst of heavy emotional reactions, and reduce strains in your relationships. Finally, you can end your suffering, recover, and reclaim your life just as many did. My greatest wish is that every reader will find some comfort in reading this book and that the grounding technique will do you as much good as it does me, every day, and many times a day.

1

THE WRONG POWER

A secret kept for too long can decay inside of you. Sometimes, we do this without meaning to. My mind kept the secret from me to the point where it created a chasm between my memories and the present. Over time, there becomes a divide between your outer identity and your inner identity. This is what happened to me.

You could say my early life was split into parts: the one before and the one after sexual abuse. Later on, when I joined some anonymous fraternities and a support group for childhood sexual abuse survivors, my life would split again. But it is the first split that created a chasm between me and my body, my mind, and my emotions. However, when relaying the full story, it's important to go back to the source: family. That's where it all begins.

When victims of terrible events speak their story, it usually starts off the same. They had a normal life, an average life, before the big event that shook their world. My story is no different. What wasn't normal was that I underwent sexual abuse during my 5th and 6th years of life. However, those memories remained stuck under the surface until the first event that would rock my reality, decades later.

I grew up in a typical 1960s household. I had a working father, the breadwinner, who secured a job as an engineer but had a tumultuous relationship with drinking, and a mother who took care of household responsibilities. We weren't religious, though, religious values were present in our everyday lifestyle.

I grew up in Quebec, a French province in Canada, which at the time was influenced strongly by Church power. By "influence," I really mean that the Church essentially took over most sectors of society, especially citizen-focused sectors. Education, social services, health services, labor unions, and so on, were the Church's responsibilities. My parents experienced this during their youth and even when they reached adulthood. Every Sunday, mass at our neighborhood Church was filled to the brim. The economic boom of the post-war period allowed many to study up to university, creating a certain middle class that wanted to get rid of the influence of the church. These elites were looking to more modern values, as opposed to the previously traditionalist values of religious Quebec. As whispers of modernity spread word of corporate wealth reached the streets.

People were freeing themselves from the hold the Church had on them. The church no longer has any influence on government decisions. By 1970, the switch had practically been completed, with most of the societal responsibilities handed over to the state.

The society that surrounds an individual is so crucial in understanding his or her experience. While our immediate family and environment affect our lives, it is the historical context that shapes them first. For me, it was this environment that would affect and exacerbate the trauma I underwent.

In our community, religious leaders were respected, idolized, and treated like royalty. Speaking negatively about them would be slander. That makes sense, doesn't it? They were pillars of moral righteousness. They were the people we should seek to emulate. Everyone trusted them because religion was the center of society. It gave the rights to the people that the evil, capitalist state government was so against. As mentioned before, religion dictated nearly all facets of life, from social welfare to education and even to worker's unions.

So, no one would ever expect a priest to, in any way, take advantage of another - least of all, child; me, a kindergartener.

I remember the priest who lived in my community, incredibly close to my school. Back then, close, tight-knit communities felt a sense of trust and security with each other. Young children were free to wander the neighborhood, seeing as everyone knew everyone. The priest near the school was known for giving out candies and treats to visiting children. One day, my cousin and I decided to take a short trip there. My cousin was only three or four years of age, and I, was two years older. We went up to his door, I knocked on her door, waited...

That's all I could remember for two decades.

There's something funny about memory when you're young. Sometimes you don't know if you can trust yourself. Our memories are not just shaped by our experiences but also by what others tell us or how we rationalize an experience. Have you ever looked through photos of yourself when you were younger, to times you could barely remember, and a parent or family member recounts to you the story behind the picture? Then, one day, years afterward, your mind constructs a memory based on the image and the family member's story. You can almost feel like you've lived through that memory, but it's based on someone else's account, not yours. It's amazing how the mind constructs a story on its mental screen. When you don't understand something, your mind simply fills in the blanks.

I had a big blank in my mind about what happened that day at the priest's house.

It wasn't until I was in my thirties, driving around doing my errands that I got a sudden flashback that uncracked the wall hiding that memory. I'll get more into that later though. The important thing is that I now know that the priest used me for sexual gratification. The important thing is the emotions that remained imprinted into my soul from that short time at his house. Confusion. Paralysis. Sickness. Disgust.

I felt things that a child cannot even wrap her head around. Emotions that I can only pair with words now. I felt used and thrown away. I felt less than human. I felt shocked to my core. I don't think my tiny developing brain could have even understood what was going on, only that it was horrid. And the priest was a monster.

That's how you know that good morals are not always learned. When even a small child can feel, with utmost certainty, the darkness in a certain action, you know that behavior is inherently immoral and inhuman.

Imagine a young, defenseless child undergoing one of the most horrible experiences known to man. The child goes home to find safety, comfort, and protection. Any protector or parent in their right mind would unconditionally take that child under their wing. Now imagine, that child goes home, and instead of finding comfort, she finds blame, rejection, and coldness. What does that do to a person? What message does that child take from life?

In short, I went home. I told my mother. She called me a liar.

I don't know how any four or five-year-old could make this up. I really don't know. It's not as if lewd media was available during that time for any small child to come across. Children learn to lie to people around them, and even then, it's easy to tell when something is true or false. Yet, my mother insisted my experience was a fabrication.

How could a priest do such a thing?

That's what I wanted to know too.

How could a parent choose a vaguely important religious man over the child they spent years of pain, sweat, and tears taking care of?

I wanted to know that too.

I was sent to my room. I stayed there for hours. I can't say what I was doing or how I was feeling. When I think back now, I feel like I can view the memory from the outside, like an observer watching a movie. I was in shock. I think my mother expected me to get over it soon and come down eventually. When I didn't, she came to me. The second she walked into my room, I felt a spark of hope. Maybe she thought things over and came to apologize. Maybe she believes me now and will take action. Really, I didn't care or know what action she could have taken. I would have been okay with a hug and reassurance.

She came closer and knelt down to my level.

"Listen. Let's not tell your father any of this, alright?"

Hope shriveled up and died in my heart. That was the beginning of my silence. We never spoke of it again. I never spoke of it again. It may not have ever even happened.

Experts believe that how a childhood sexual assault is addressed imme-diately, by the adults around, is the biggest predictor of how bad the consequences will be.

By doing nothing, my mother did the worst thing she could have done to me. I received the message loud and clear. Even if I say the truth, the people who matter the most won't listen. Even in times of the worst emotional turmoil and pain, without any mental resources to help me, I will not even have the support of the people who matter the most. What I feel matters less than the worth of a stranger. I shouldn't trust myself because even my mother didn't trust me.

These are the beliefs that implanted themselves in my subconscious.

After the Quiet Revolution, the influence and the glorification of reli-gious leaders had lessened.

By then, however, the damage was done. Like everyone else, my mother was a devout supporter of the Church. Religion was normal for me when I was growing up, even though I didn't intellectually understand it. During my darkest hour, religion became associated with betrayal, resentment, and invalidation, because when I approached my religious mother to tell her my truth, she rejected it. Why? Well, my abuser was a man of the Church. How dare I make terrible falsehoods about a religious man?

I couldn't help but wonder how things would have been if I had been born a decade later. How would my mother have treated the issue if we had lived together after the Revolution after the Church gradually declined in power? It's incredible how much of a difference a few years can make. While I wish the situation had never happened, if it had even happened in the 1970s versus the 1960s, perhaps my mother would have approached it differently. Maybe she would have had more faith in me than in some man she knew nothing about but his religious affiliation. Thoughts like these always come and go, but I know that, at the end of the day, my mother's belief in my words was less than the control that the environment and society had over her. That hurts the most.

When I was 8 years old, my mother died of breast cancer. She was young, only 39 years old, and it left my family upended. My father now had to take the wheel, and in actuality, he did his best. He created a routine that worked for us. During the week, we were boarders. Over the weekend, we went back home. It was spaghetti on Saturdays, stew on Sundays, and the expectation of what was to come helped ground us despite our grief. On the surface, my siblings and I had a good time with my father.

Beneath the surface, I was repressing my emotions. All this time, the secret of my sexual abuse was kept with me without my knowledge or choice. Yet my body couldn't keep up with my mental walls. The years following my mother's death were full of sickness. I was vomiting regularly, to the point where only bile came out. Physical pain plagued my stomach, but no one knew why.

Everything changed when my father remarried. They met at work. She was someone who never had children, so joining the family gave her the role of savior, rather than just a stepmother. Understandably, at that time, single fathers would remarry to provide their children with a mother figure to help carry the parenting responsibility. However, my father's new wife contributed to a dysfunctional home environment. Each of my siblings coped in a different way, and I coped by working to get out of there as soon as possible.

The loss of my mother gave me resounding grief for years afterward. Part of it was because of my father's insistence on not holding a funeral service that could allow me to get through the stages of grief in a healthy manner. Instead, they remained stuck and suspended within me. I also suspect that I held on to the pain of my mother's death for another purpose: to mask the residual emotions and the memories of my sexual abuse. While the grief was certainly real and painful, my mind made it my focus for so long in order to keep myself safe from approaching the raw trauma buried deep in my subconscious depths. It protected me from having to address the resentment towards my mother for not believing me, and for invalidating my experience.

Because of this emotional mask, I couldn't access my memories of abuse for over two decades. Moreover, my mother's distrust in me made me question my own perception over time. Unconsciously, my mind came to believe that I had made it up because someone I held to great authority told me so. As such, my brain blocked the abuse from my brain for a long time.

However, my memories were like items that sank to the bottom of the ocean, lost to the waves. Their essence will always remain in the water that splashes against the land, and that's what happened in my adult life. My trauma haunted me in the ways that it could: through the psychological and physical consequences that became the bane of my existence.

2

CONSEQUENCES OF SEXUAL ABUSE

Just because an event happened in childhood does not mean adulthood erases it from memory. For many, the mental memories may block the details of sexual abuse. For others, the mental images are seared into the screen of their minds. What many don't consider is the ability of the body's physiology to store trauma. As a victim of childhood sexual abuse goes through adolescence and adulthood, this trauma manifests through a diverse set of signs and symptoms.

According to the INSPQ, there is a plethora of consequences of abuse, including:

- Depression

- Anxiety

- Low sense of self

- Alcoholism

- Gambling

- Drug abuse & addiction

- Behavioral problems

- Developmental delays

- Social anxiety

- Post-traumatic stress disorder symptoms

- Dissociation

- Risk-taking behavior

- Self-harm

- Suicidal ideation

The effects of childhood sexual abuse can show up in complex ways. It is difficult to define where some of our most self-destructive habits come from. A lot of the consequences listed above can be attributed to other factors too, like social class, racial inequity, location, family genetics, community, and so on. It's important to go a bit more in-depth into how these symptoms manifest in the body and mind of an abuse survivor.

For women, adulthood can follow the dark past with a slew of physical health effects, particularly in the abdominal area and reproductive organs. They can struggle with their sexuality, an issue that can go in either direction: lack of arousal during intimacy or overexpression of arousal. In other words, some survivors may struggle to feel the personal physical desire that is separated from their association with abuse. Alternatively, some women may actually feel hypersexual, leading to risk-taking behavior, coupling with multiple partners in their lifetime, and thus, potentially being at risk for STIs.

Physically, survivors may feel vague pain in their stomach area, like I did, or they may have pelvic pain. Overall, many of us might have either a lower pain threshold, which simply means we are more sensitive to pain and sensation than others, or some may have a high pain threshold, after a childhood trying to undertake the hurt of physical abuse in an effort to feel some sort of control.

Now, let's talk about the emotional and psychological effects of childhood sexual abuse. Firstly, it's common for survivors to struggle with healthy interpersonal connections. Because of trauma, their walls are always up, on guard, in case someone else betrays them once again. So they may keep themselves isolated and alone in an effort to avoid further pain, which of course sacrifices the potential for positive human connection. Others may victimize themselves again and again.... not on purpose, but as an expression of the trauma that happened to them. Their innocence was shattered as a child, and they never learned the right way to defend themselves from the predators that initially preyed on them.

Their trauma broke down their sense of self and worthiness, and now they believe that they do not deserve respect beyond what they received during the incident that caused their trauma. Another explanation is that they mentally normalized that experience, in an effort to survive. Trauma can be so devastating that the child's brain tries to shield itself by making the experience fit some sort of twisted logic. Adults around during that time make the problem worse by gaslighting the victim or blaming them, forcing them to feel deserving of that level of disrespect for years after it's all said and done. The thing is that how a survivor interacts with others and functions through adult life is not out of choice; it all happens unconsciously, without their awareness of what they are doing. Before they know it, they have a trail of toxic relationships, all the time believing that they are the problem.

Alongside interpersonal issues, many survivors are at risk of post-traumatic stress disorder symptoms, depression, and anxiety. With PTSD comes the classic flashbacks, nightmares, disassociation, and hypervigilance. These symptoms can get out of control and severely cause dysfunction in a person's life, especially when triggered by unexpected or uncontrollable factors. Even without these symptoms, survivors tend to repeatedly feel strong emotional responses to seemingly normal things, like a high amount of shame or humiliation for no exact reason. Guilt and low self-worth seem to be a normal part of an abused victim's adult life. They might over-apologize or assume nobody likes them, even if others continually give them signs of affection and love, and validation. In other words, their view of themselves can be so incredibly distorted and unrealistic. It's almost self-dysphoric. What they think of themselves is so far removed from who they actually are or seem to other people.

This dysphoria can also translate to an unhealthy perspective of their own body. Many survivors of childhood sexual abuse can struggle with connecting with their bodies. Part of this is due to the state of disassociation they are used to entering. Another part of it is that at some point in childhood, usually during the traumatic event, they disconnect from their body to reduce the horror of the experience. Unfortunately, these survival mechanisms remain during adulthood, and it can make it difficult for someone to watch out for and listen to their bodily cues. As such, they can struggle with remaining present, they can struggle with hunger signals and eating patterns, and even develop an eating disorder to cope. Eating disorders for many sexual abuse survivors are a way for a person to take back some sort of control over their bodies.

A combination of the horrid emotional repercussions and physical pains leaves survivors vulnerable to substance use and abuse. Adults who have experienced abuse of any kind in childhood are 4-5 times more likely to pick up a substance abuse disorder along the way. Be it drugs, alcohol, or smoking, survivors try to fill the emptiness within.

At least, that's what I did.

My past led to a strong dependence on alcohol. At first, I thought I was just doing what everyone else did: enjoying a drink, then a couple more. I didn't attribute it to self-medicating or using it to forget my trauma. Before I knew it, one drink led to another, and it wasn't enough. Eventually, I got to the point where as soon as I had a drink, I felt the urge to seek love from someone -- but not just love, I wanted it without attachment, without commitment. In other words, without alcohol, I struggled with intimacy and personal relationships. With it, all my inhibitions lowered, and the desire I suppressed daily surfaced.

Alcohol had a more sinister connection to my victimization. It was both my cure and my poison. I used it to forget, but it was also used against me to place me in traumatic situations. When I was a child, my aunt -- my mother's sister -- had a husband who was undergoing his doctoral studies. He was a psychology student and asked my mother's permission for me to participate in one of his studies. I was young, but I still remember going to the university and sitting at a small, kid-sized table. At the time, I didn't really get what was going on. I remember him asking me questions about geometric shapes. I remember him taking me back home. I remember him giving me something to drink, after which I felt woozy. That's when the holes in my memory began. However, I can still vaguely remember what he did to me, and the act left a mark that would affect the rest of my education and adult life.

Ironically, this doctoral student reported to my parents the results of the study I underwent. According to him, I had above-average intelligence. This should have been good news, and I did believe it, all the while aiming to forget what happened. Or rather, my child-self simply put the memory of the abuse on the back burner, not sure how to categorize it. I was confused, didn't know what to make of it. My body, though, knew exactly what it had gone through. Because of this moment, my body would reject the idea of higher education, making it uncomfortable for me to pursue it. I couldn't attend university until I was 23 years old, and even then, I felt so behind the other students, most of whom were 18-19 years old. How could I supposedly have above-average intelligence, yet still struggle in academic environments? It sparked my inferiority complex and destroyed my self-esteem.

I also struggled with keeping a job. Unemployment and job instability are common consequences of childhood abuse. Despite having a few interesting positions, I didn't stick around long. I had little motivation, mainly because I couldn't see what my future held. I didn't know what I wanted to do or aspire to become, and I had trouble expressing my desires if I had any. Because I took interactions so seriously, jobs were more stressful for me than the average person. It was a challenge to trust my coworkers, my boss, and my customers. I couldn't feel comfortable enough at any job to work to the best ability or at least work without debilitating anxiety. Normal situations would anger me to a disproportionate degree, and the emotional toll was exhausting.

Through all this, alcohol would become my crutch. I'm not sure if I subconsciously chose it to have more control over the weapon involved with my trauma or if it was available at the most convenient of times. Regardless of why alcohol is one of the most "socially acceptable" forms of self-destructive coping mechanisms. It doesn't carry the stigma of smoking tobacco or hard drugs. As such, when I tried to get help for my trauma, most therapies didn't offer support for or address substance abuse. The issue with group therapy, which is available and preferred for people who don't have the money or insurance to spend on private, individual long-term therapy, is that mental health issues are dealt with separately. What is more likely is that a person's set of mental health concerns and behavioral problems may be linked and affect each other. One self-destructive habit may manifest in response to another core mental health concern. For instance, a person struggling with binge eating disorder, and Complex PTSD (C-PTSD), might seek services to address each of those separately. Or maybe they have just enough time and availability to join a C-PTSD group therapy. In therapy, they never bring up their eating issues because they think it is irrelevant or a self-control issue. Unfortunately, that perspective tends to be incorrect. What's more likely is that their binge eating disorder manifested to deal with their C-PTSD, which stems from long-term traumatic experiences. Thus, both must be handled simultaneously.

That's the issue with recovering from the trauma that can lead to a network of different negative consequences. Some people say you have to get to the root of the problem in order to deal with the effects. In this case, the root would be childhood sexual abuse, and the consequences are substance and alcohol abuse. However, what if these "consequences" are actually creating a barrier between you and your potential to heal? What if you actually can't get to the root because your subconscious has created a series of protective defenses to keep you and others out? Alcohol is a coping mechanism, and as long as you are only coping, you cannot be healing. It's like a bandage rather than a cure. In order to truly cure yourself, you need to rip off the bandage, address the injury, dab some antibacterial ointment in there, and let it burn, until the inflammation dies down, and the wound can finally begin mending itself.

When it comes to people with both substance abuse disorders and childhood trauma (of any kind), it's strongly recommended that they address the former first. Alcohol and drugs offer a clear purpose for victims of trauma, and that is to keep the challenging feelings and memories at bay. If you think about it, substances are a way to perpetuate dissociative habits. When emotions or feelings become challenging, they escape by turning to substances. They don't know how to approach uncomfortable topics sober. This will prevent actual progress from occurring.

That's why many PTSD therapy programs do not allow individuals to join until they have detoxed and abstained from a substance. There are some treatment models that allow for the intervention of acute trauma symptoms initially, to give the individual a leg-up when they have to quit the substance. After all, forcing a person to abstain from the one thing that may be holding them back from distressing symptoms, dysfunction, or even suicidal ideation can be cruel. In general, though, for a person to really get to the thick of their trauma, ceasing their self-medication is necessary. For one, those substances may be warping the individual's judgment and memory further. They can barely remember what they ate for dinner last night. How can they reach into their minds for a traumatic memory in childhood?

Secondly, addiction can be a crutch that a person can use as an excuse to not work on their healing. It can be a tempting tool to avoid going through the work of learning actual grounding techniques. We've all been there. Things get really bad and we finally feel desperate for a solution. Then, the wave of despair might pass for a short while, and we fall into complacency. We wonder if we're actually in that bad of a place. Maybe I'm actually not struggling that bad; maybe I can keep doing this. If things do get bad, a nice drink will do the trick. It's really easy for us to trick ourselves when we're not looking at the bigger picture. All this is to say that if you want to recover from childhood sexual abuse, it's so important that you seek help for your addiction or substance use first. For some, it's drugs or alcohol. Some may even depend heavily on caffeine, stimulants, energy drinks, etc. Whatever you depend on to get through the day, you need to address it in order to face the demons within.

If you are looking for alcohol or substance abuse programs, keep this in mind. Because topic-based therapy models are created separately, they may not take into account the different nuances or needs of trauma-based mental health concerns. What I mean by this is that survivors of childhood sexual trauma may be overly sensitive to certain parts of the narrative involved in the 12-step model. For alcohol and substance abuse, the 12-step model exists to systematically lead an individual toward recovering from their dependence. It has shown a beneficial impact on many patients and clients. However, many 12-step programs support a narrative of "giving in," of accepting one's "powerlessness." More religion-based programs might even include the wording of "letting go of control to a higher power" or "surrendering." For victims of any sort of abuse, particularly sexual abuse, this narrative can be harmful and terrifying. We've lived our entire lives at the mercy of "higher powers." In our minds, we feel lower than anything and anyone else in this world. We are trying to gain that power and control back, to feel more secure in ourselves and our lives. The idea of giving in may be freeing to people who have not undergone childhood trauma. It may help them feel more accepting of life's harshness and become more resilient. However, this idea can have the opposite effect on survivors of childhood sexual abuse.

What is essential is that you vet the available 12-step programs in your area first to find one that is sensitive to the different experiences of individuals. Then, make sure you don't stop there. For me, the 12-step group therapy worked to solve my alcohol addiction and survive for several years. I was even able to break up with a relationship of betrayal that had lasted for 6 years. I learned to admit my wrongs and be honest with myself. I put my family relationships in order. I acquired a certain discipline at home. However, in my affective relationships and with my colleagues, I always felt in search of approval and comfort. I quickly fell into my emotions of anger and rage when things didn't go the way I wanted. My reactions to these issues led me again to lose a very interesting job and to alienate the emotional relationship that I held so dear. The women's group therapy is what helped more because it specifically dealt with the wounds left by the trauma. A support group with a professional trained in childhood sexual abuse is crucial because it comprehends the distinct consequences of this sort of background.

In any case, it's important to build awareness of how your trauma has affected your life. Understanding the consequences and reflecting on how they manifest for you is key to knowing what your goals are in the healing process. That's what I had to do, and I decided to begin with my relationship issues.

3

BEFORE REMEMBERING

Childhood sexual abuse and memory loss go hand-in-hand. Many victims barely remember what they went through until adulthood. Usually, that happens when something familiar or relevant to the memory triggers it.

Memory loss is very common, but why? Because blocking out memories is how the developing brain copes with trauma. Others who experienced constant childhood abuse may find a whole chunk of their childhood years vague and inaccessible. All this is to protect your still-growing mind from its own pain. While that's all fine and dandy, it can also make you struggle to believe in yourself. You may doubt that you ever lived through the trauma that your memories hint at. Other people can help you gaslight yourself by not believing you or questioning your reality, of which you don't have a stable foundation.

This specific memory loss is called dissociative amnesia. It describes the state in which you cannot bring to the forefront very critical memories in your life, that anyone should be able to remember. Dissociative amnesia actually leads to more forgotten memories than normal. It is the reason that you may have holes in your memory, an inability to think back to specific details about your life, or your traumatic situation. Other times, you might think back to your memories from an outside point of view. For example, you might see yourself from the third person. Whatever the case, dissociative amnesia is a trauma response that aids in helping a young person continue to function.

Before I remembered the events that led to my trauma, I only experienced the consequences and knew something was wrong. According to research, negative or traumatic childhood experiences can result in a higher risk of health problems. Instead of emotional pain, the trauma is translated physically, making your body and brain undergo difficulty so long as your psyche doesn't face the truth, which could destroy you while you are still young and unprepared.

However, as an adult, those consequences of trauma that once protected you are now keeping you in a pigeonhole. The coping mechanisms that once helped you as a child are now keeping you from living life to the fullest as an adult. You can feel trapped by your own self. It feels like a prison created by your own hands. How do you escape a hell you've continued to perpetuate?

When I was sick of going through the same patterns of self-destructive behavior, I knew I had to try something new. My financial stability was shaky, my job fulfillment nonexistent, and my life purposeless. My relationship with my family was fleeting and still tense with the weight of unaddressed emotional issues. My personal relationships and dating life were problematic. While learning behavioral and life skills would help, something within me was blocking me from success in any of these areas. It was deeper than learning how to communicate, or a what healthy relationship looks like. I knew I needed healing.

Luckily, I could at least have a level of awareness that allowed me to identify my main issues. I had a substance abuse problem. I ran away from my feelings. I used relationships to fill a void. I still was avoiding my mother's death. I still struggled with shame and self-worth. Awareness of what my problems were -- and acceptance of them -- gave me the push to seek further support. Anonymous fraternities weren't enough. The women's support group was immensely helpful, but I would have never been able to open up to it if I didn't solve my problems with substance abuse.

Healing is a long journey, and I learned this the hard way. While I had a lot of areas to take care of, it was impossible to do them all. So I chose two areas that I figured I should tackle first: Adaptation and interpersonal relationships.

I began by seeking help with my difficulty in adapting to situations.

Adaptation is a funny thing when it comes to abuse and trauma. Traumatic responses are how the brain and body adapt to incredibly stressful situations in childhood. However, those adaptation habits can make actually adapting to stressful adult situations even harder than they are for the average person.

Here's one example: Programmed silence is one such adaptation that many survivors of trauma face. When stressed or under pressure, a person may simply fall silent and refuse to speak or express himself. Many people have a mild expression of this, as seen in those who prefer to not talk when upset or angry. Survivors of childhood trauma may take this adaptation habit of silence to an extreme degree, refusing to offer their true thoughts or opinions in even the most harmless of situations. This habit of remaining silent falls under the category of the *freeze* response. In fact, many adaptation habits are rooted in the four traumatic responses: Fight, Flight, Freeze, or Fawn.

Fighters respond to high-stress or dangerous situations with aggression. Flighters run away or avoid the stressor. Freezers basically stop in place and shut down mentally and emotionally. Fawners respond by appeasing the source of stress, not in a manipulative way, but more by submitting to the situation to avoid pain. While helpful in some cases, or out in the wilderness, these trauma responses can actually cause more problems. In adulthood, the fawn response can look like people pleasing, which can lead to lower boundaries and decreased self-respect. The freeze response can look like the way I mentioned before, with being unable to speak for yourself because you are so terrified you can't speak or move. The fight response can look like uncontrollable angry outbursts and feeling defensive at any little act, leading to conflict and anger management problems. The flight response can look like a number of avoidance tactics, like self-isolation, distraction with substances, or addictive activity.

Many people may have a mixture of these responses. Even "healthier" people who are not struggling with immense psychological trouble from trauma can show milder forms of these responses. The problem is when they are so ingrained and automatic that you cannot adapt to situations in a healthy manner. This is what happened to me. Any little change in my life shook me up, and I didn't have the proper tools to cope with them, much less adapt. Trauma can mess with a person's ability to be resilient. And I wanted to be resilient.

As for relationship irregularities, that's a no-brainer. But it helps to see why many survivors of childhood sexual trauma tend to struggle with relationships. Relational challenges can consist of everything from our personal connections with the people in our lives to how we relate with other people. Such challenges can affect work, family, and social spheres. It can look like many things. You may struggle with confronting people or simply having any conversation beneath the surface level. You may feel social anxiety, not because you are shy or insecure, but because of a mysterious discomfort you have with others. Often, this discomfort is a result of your hyperactive defense system. Many survivors of childhood trauma (of any kind, really) tend to be overly sensitive to tiny signs in their environment. A slight downward tilt of the eyebrow or a change in posture can alert their defense system that something is wrong, that someone is angry with them, which can lead to a series of misunderstandings. This defense system isn't the most accurate, because it can lead to a dissolution of one's personal will and sense of self. Their behaviors become dictated by how they feel others feel, which means they prioritize their perception of others over their own desires and needs. Usually, such people are overly empathic, but that empathy is not helpful to either them or others, because it leads to people-pleasing behavior or to drawing away from potential relationships. The truth of the matter is that healthy relationships have a balance of both people's needs, cooperation, and sacrifices. Conflicts will come, and avoiding them by being "perfect" and never causing another person inconveniences is not the way to a genuine relationship.

Another relational issue is an inability to set boundaries. While some survivors are hyper-aware of other people's body language, others actually feel more comfortable with people and situations that are most likely to take advantage of them. A person who has undergone childhood abuse may be more likely to feel "at home" with people who remind her unconsciously of that situation.

Finally, another common relational challenge is the ability to connect, sympathize, and even empathize with people. Don't misunderstand; this is not because traumatized individuals lack empathy. Rather, it's because of the symptoms and consequences of trauma: the dissociation, the fear, the self-blame and self-focus, the negative self-image, anxiety, and addictive coping mechanisms. These things can make it harder to be present in relationships and to see others' perspectives in a way that does not put the blame on us. For instance, you might be able to sympathize with a friend going through difficulty, but it's hard because clouding your mind is the fear that it's your fault your friend is distant.

While these relational difficulties can affect your emotional health and social life, since all humans need a connection to survive, they can also get in the way of work life. For instance, you might be unable to negotiate or communicate with coworkers. You might struggle to approach your manager or boss to have difficult conversations that might be crucial to your well-being in the workplace or your career. Understanding why other people do certain things can be hard, leading to you taking many

things personally in a professional setting. This can be a troubling experience because you receive a greater emotional charge than you should be
carrying at your job. A lot of the time, our low self-esteem and habit of
blaming ourselves can make us assume that a coworker's words or actions
are about us personally. Finally, operating in a team or hierarchy can be
difficult overall. Many survivors of childhood sexual trauma can struggle
to separate their powerlessness in childhood from the power relations at
work, and it can be triggering on a daily basis.

For these ailments, I started attending group therapy. For a year and a few
months, I gathered with the same group of people, four meetings a week.
We had a system where anyone could express what they were experiencing
at that moment or discuss their issues based on pre-determined themes.

The issue with self-healing is that you can't trust yourself. While group
therapy is a supportive environment, no one is forcing you to say anything. Each person has a responsibility to themselves to express themselves. What that also meant is that sometimes people cheat. Take me
for example. One of the highlights of my painful past was my mother's
death, a wound that never had a chance to heal. Yet, I did not mention it
in group therapy until after half a year of meetings.

To say the group was stunned is an understatement.

By that time in the group, it was uncalled-for for such a huge loss in someone's life to not be mentioned. If I had been in individual therapy, my therapist probably would have wondered why it took so long for me to bring up my mother's death. Even though I was young when it happened, most people tend to discuss major family deaths earlier in the sessions, because it plays a big role in their life.

As for me, it was a closed file. I had never expressed anything related to it before in life, not even in childhood. That's unusual for children. Even if the grief is difficult, young children are not so stringent about keeping in details about their life. The support group was the first time I felt safe discussing it.

So I started talking. However, I was ignoring another important factor that affected me. The support group unfortunately did not address alcohol use. Although it advocated for a drug-free approach, alcohol outside of therapy was allowed to the participants. I didn't think it would be relevant to discuss my alcohol issues at the time. Now I understand that although I thought I was forthcoming and honest, that honesty was omitting a critical detail. Only because of this did I leave therapy with the same inner baggage.

That baggage was clear in how many families continued to operate in adulthood. Up until this point, I had an unusual relationship with my family. Ever since I left them after high school, I avoided family meetings. I only saw them at special events, like birthdays and Christmas. Although my siblings and I were all affected by our mother's death, no one talked about it, and that had yet to change. So even though I let off some of my grief during therapy, I still had unfinished business. It felt like my family and I had to open up about the issue together.

Of course, there were other things that also affected my relationship with my family. For one, I felt ashamed for not having a decent job. I often had long periods of unemployment. The jobs I could hold were contract work that I ended up leaving because I had little ambition or motivation to continue.

For another, I also felt ashamed of my dating life. It was hard to face my family when so many facets of my life were in shambles, even though it's true that no one has it all together. I kept up a long-term relationship in which I was not comfortable. The only thing I liked about it was the sexual part. However, even that was a mess. The boyfriend at the time would cheat on me with other women, and I still stayed, even though I knew this. Eventually, he contracted an STD. Somehow, this wasn't the last straw for me. He had the nerve to put me in charge of the financial situation, paying for rent, food, and medical bills. I thought the STD made him learn his lesson, though, so I continued to give him a chance. After several months of dating without any issues, he proposed to me, and we moved in together. The day I moved in, I remember I had a sore throat so bad I couldn't swallow, yet he told me to stop complaining with contempt in his voice. This was the first red flag, in my eyes, but I put it behind me because we'd been planning to move in for a while. I reasoned that it was such a big life change, so feeling hurt from his words seemed like too little a reason to call everything off.

For two months of living together, I felt empty. Quickly, a fear was dawning on me that I had made a mistake. I felt like I was playing a role. I was getting so lost in the relationship that I didn't feel like myself. Yet, I remained hanging on to a relationship that was not even passing the bare minimum standards.

One day, the phone rang. My boyfriend (or fiancé) wasn't home, so I answered.

It was a woman.

She said she was waiting for my boyfriend to visit her. She wanted to tell me that he was seeing her. Even though he and I were living together, even though we had gone to the next step, he still managed to cheat on me again. I thought we had overcome his infidelity issues, but I supposed it was only a matter of time. That was the final straw for me: I moved out.

I realized I was repeating the same victim's behaviors. Now, I realize that my ex had a lot more red flags from the very beginning, from the first sense of discomfort I felt. If not, then from the first time he cheated on me. However, my judgment could easily brush off the problems by focusing on the little positive things that I thought were worthwhile. By the time the relationship had passed the long-term stage, I figured I could look past his flaws since we'd known each for so long. Looking back, I deserved much more, but I could not see that.

When I moved out, I stayed with a friend who I met in therapy. After a short time living together, my roommate had a good idea: To join an anonymous group for alcohol addiction. She was struggling with alcohol addiction. She asked me to join her. I agreed. By accompanying her to make an appointment, I feel like I mentally and spiritually ended the unhealthy relationship with my cheating ex. It was over. I never saw him again. Joining the Alcoholics Anonymous group was like starting a new chapter in my life.

This rollercoaster of a failed relationship and almost marriage left me embarrassed when family members asked me questions about my dating life. But, they understood.

Later, I met a guy through my sister. He was caring, affectionate, and nice. I learned that he also had drug problems. Eventually, I attended anonymous group meetings with him. Soon, as I got to know more about him, I eventually moved in with him. It was a short period of blissful happiness.

The period ended when I realized I was repeating the same mistakes, seeking and staying with people who were just as broken as I was. We had a connection, but if I learned anything from past relationships, it was that the people I attracted were either emotionally unavailable or emotionally pained. That was no fault of his, of course. I knew what I was getting into when I found out he struggled with drugs. However, the beginning stages of a relationship are so bright and full of hope. I forgot how hard it was to fall in love with someone with an addiction. Being someone with a dependence on alcohol, I knew I wasn't the easiest to love.

Long story short, I couldn't keep a job, and he was using drugs too much. His usage was draining our finances and his mental stability. We were both suffering and hiding that suffering with substance use. Our brief happiness dissolved into misery. Our own demons stopped us from living well, even though we could have made a great team together.

Just when I was thinking about leaving him, he took his life.

There is a bittersweet mixture of pain and guilt and grief that you feel when someone dear to you commits suicide. Firstly, I lost someone dear to me. Despite the troubles in life, a person's essence still remains shining brightly in my heart. Love or not, he had come to be important to me, and now he was gone forever. I wouldn't get to see him again, not to break up, not to see him potentially heal his drug problem. It destroyed me, to see potential and hope disintegrate into nothing. Moreover, the guilt ate at me. Even though I knew it wasn't my fault, that in the end, it was his choice to make, I still felt responsible. I felt like I could have done more or been more supportive. Was there anything I could have done? Or was my rumination just an attempt to feel more in control of the situation? I didn't know. It also made me realize that no matter what you do, you may not be able to help another. You could live more gently, more kindly, and try to support others in the best way you can. Your words and actions may influence them and be a strong factor in their choices. However, you are only responsible for yourself. I was responsible for myself and my healing. No one was going to save me, just as I couldn't save him.

His death was a wake-up call for me. I realized the depth of mortality and how close death was, to all of us. Even if I was stable one day, I might end up in a similar mental state another day. Or I might lose my life in an accident. In other words, I truly felt what it meant when we say, "you don't live forever," or "you only live once." It was a heavy reminder that my current pain and struggle were not worth drowning in alcohol; I still had a chance to get out. If I didn't, it would be disrespectful to my boyfriend's death, in a way.

It was this brutal end that prompted me to continue to attend Alcoholics Anonymous meetings with greater fervor and try to fix my alcohol abuse for good. If I couldn't help another, I could at least help myself. I found comfort in meetings. I didn't feel alone with people who, regardless of what they were numbing with their alcohol, had that in common with me.

I've now been sober since 1996.

Finally, I met another man at an AA meeting. I felt a strong bond with him, not just because of the similar struggles from which we were healing. As I got to know him more, we began dating and would eventually enter a steady relationship. He already had kids, and while I was nervous at first, they welcomed me and I felt at home with them. While the relationship wasn't always easy, we had a very happy, relatively stable time together. I loved it most when we were living together with his children in shared custody. They were some of the best years of my life. I kept a job for over 4 years, which was a record for me. Everything was looking up.

After several years of going steady, things began to change. I had a hard time adjusting. I knew changes would come eventually, but I didn't realize that they would all come at once. My spouse's children were all grown up and ready to move out to live their own lives. The house had to be sold, and my spouse could afford a house to his liking, but it was far from my job, which I was adamant to keep. Not to mention, I was beginning to have health problems, so I wasn't able to provide the energy for a full-time job, much less a long commute. As a temporary solution, I had to stay in an apartment while my spouse bought the house he desired in the country.

I have to admit, I was angry at the situation. The anger brought up feelings of resentment and grief for my mother, like a trigger. It was like my betrayal wound was activated. I wished my spouse could have seen my side, and put me first, just as I wished my mother would have put me first over my religious, respected abusers. I was her daughter. How could she have turned me away?

Instead of going back to my unhealthy coping mechanisms, I stopped and thought about my state in life. I knew logically that my spouse was making a logical choice. This situation, although difficult, would not be like this forever. I had surpassed many other difficulties in life, and I could overcome this as well. However, I had to do something about the emotions arising. They were a sign of my younger self's unhealed pain. I finally decided the time away from my spouse was perfect for taking the chance to finally grieve for my mother. I probably could not have done it in the relationship, because it was a place of comfort that I would turn to for escape.

To fully grieve, I had a headstone made for my mother. I let out all my feelings about her without being capsized or ripped apart. I talked of her and to her. Mentally, I gave her a eulogy. I let myself sob over her death. I cried about her betrayal. When the period was over, and I felt I had nothing more to clear from my mind, I moved back in with my spouse.

I think that clearing up the blockage in the grief towards my mother's death finally opened up the path to remembering the abuse that it had been protecting me from. The mind and emotions always do things for a reason. Think about it as levels of consciousness. As you heal and unblock something negative from your consciousness, you unlock another, deeper level of consciousness that may provide you with darker parts of your emotions and memories. Before, you weren't ready to face them. But when you make enough progress, you are ready to go to the next level and overcome it too, because you are mentally prepared, no matter how horrible it is. That's what happened to me: Two decades after the abuse, I *remembered.*

4

TUMULTUOUS RELATIONSHIPS

As mentioned in the consequences, many victims of childhood sexual abuse struggle with relationships. Complicated and unstable emotional bonds mark my life, from adolescence to adulthood. When I was younger, in our middle-class community, I struggled to make friends or date. Once I left home, after high school, I was really surviving, not thriving. My trauma, even if it wasn't that clear to me in my mind, dictated my every move. I was acting like the world was a harsh jungle, a war zone, in which I could trust nobody. I had my guard up wherever I went since my childhood innocence and trust were shattered prematurely.

The difficulty of making friends would follow me through adulthood. At 19 years of age, I was severe in my ties. If I felt betrayed, I cut things off.

This was regardless of whether a person actually meant to break my trust or not. If I even *felt* a sign of distrust, emotionally, things were over. In other words, I was the one with the challenge of letting people in. I didn't think I was the problem; I just couldn't stay when I sensed even an ounce of negativity. Indeed, many of my platonic and romantic relationships were filled with negative emotions that colored even the good times. In time, I saw that it could be traced to my low self-esteem and a deep well of guilt that I could never seem to identify. I'd feel guilty for not being a good friend, or for exhibiting toxic behaviors toward my exes. Or sometimes, I'd be guilty for no reason at all.

Because of my low self-worth, I didn't seek relationships beyond what I thought I deserved, subconsciously. When I finally got sick of feeling these overwhelming emotions, I turned to alcohol.

Alcohol allowed me to be more in control, ironically enough. Sure, it let down many of my defenses and allowed me to be more open with people. But more than that, it helped me stomp down on those uncomfortable emotions that plagued me. The guilt, anxiety, shame, and rage: drinking hid it all, from myself and from others. It got to the point where I "needed" to drink in order to live and have fun, enjoy my early adult years, and even create a social circle, albeit small.

Most of my friends at the time, I made in bars. It was perfect: go to drink, lower my inhibitions, block the negative emotions, and welcome social interaction. The perfect package. Bars were where I had not only found drinking buddies and dancing buddies, but also dates. I won't lie, it was fun. However, the good times were unequally rivaled by the bad. Unfortunately, being drunk a lot of the time messed with my overall memories. So, I wouldn't realize my bad judgment when meeting people, until years later after some reflection. From what I do remember from when I was sober, I experienced the negative aspects of my relationships clearly. My friendships were tinged with negativity. For instance, one friend's brother tried to rape me while I was completely drunk. We were roommates at the time, and she threw me out on the street later in our relationship. Why? She thought I wanted to sleep with her boyfriend.

Other than alcohol clouding my judgment, why did I attract myself to similar people? Many of the women were just like me in some way or another: broken, betrayed, lost, and seeking love and validation. Others were led by self-destructive behaviors in an effort to claim more control over their bodies and autonomy. Often, those behaviors would also be factors in victimizing them.

For example, one girl I knew worked as a dancer. I met her when she was dating a friend of my boyfriend. Months after breaking up with her boyfriend, we lost sight of each other for a while. Then she called me back to tell me that she had started doing that which she had tried to avoid for as long as possible: become a dancer in a bar. I didn't understand what I found in common with such a person. I had other friends with similar jobs; one was also a dancer in a strip club and another was repeatedly sexually assaulted over and over. I had two other friends who were drunk all the time. In other words, I was surrounded by people who had suffered. I had an inexplicable connection or attraction to them; it was outside of my conscious awareness. At the same time, I judged them to an extent -- I will be honest. The friends that I invited into my life, whom I matched with on an energetic level, I also perceived with less sympathy than I should have. I can only attribute this to projecting my own rejection of my feelings of shame, of needing external validation, of lacking security and trust. I didn't accept my own state of being, and that translated over to how I viewed others. Many of my so-called friends were also struggling inside, just like me. When we came together, we just masked it all with crazy outings drinking and dancing, and risk-taking behavior. It wasn't healthy. Nor was it sustainable.

My friendships were shallow and short-lived. My romantic relationships were tumultuous. Most of this was due to my internal drives pushing me to carry out coping mechanisms, like disconnecting from my emotions outside of my conscious control. I had several issues that I acted out repeatedly and notoriously in dating. I was afraid of commitment, unwilling to risk greater pain and betrayal. I could not imagine myself investing in a love that had even the tiniest likelihood of failure. I was also uncertain that I had the capacity to give someone else commitment. The responsibility seemed too big a burden to carry. It didn't feel like the beautiful, secure, lovely thing that healthy people discussed when talking about long-term relationships. To me, it felt like a prison, like being trapped. I never wanted to feel stuck or attached to something, even if deep down, I did crave affection and intimacy. I wanted to remain free, and committing to a relationship was out of the question. I thought I could get the validation I wanted through one-night stands and temporary flings, by being in control of my love life. I made moves as I saw fit and drew away when things felt too serious. Most of these "moves" were made while drunk, and I was able to allow myself to seek others and cling to them.

Apparently, these fears and neuroses are normal among survivors of sexual abuse, in childhood or otherwise. Part of it is that, because of your trauma, you are wary of putting yourself in a vulnerable position again. As such, you will navigate relationships with push and pull -- you will try to seek the love you want, but the prospect of getting too close will fill you with anxiety and hold you back. You might pull away from your partner, end the relationship, or lash out. Another aspect of it is that trauma can severely damage your sense of self-worth. Many victims do not feel deserving of a level of healthy, respectful love. Instead, they will unconsciously attract relationships in which they are treated at the level they think matches their self-worth. They may feel inherently unlovable or rejected. It can be hard for them to believe that they can receive proper, loving treatment from others. That's not to say that they are to blame for the situations they end up in. Instead, the trauma can be so pervasive that it affects a person's thoughts, beliefs, emotions, and behaviors, leading them to make unhelpful and even dangerous decisions at times. If they do not become aware of these issues, it can be difficult to snap out of them and heal.

Shame is also a big factor in dating and relationships. Survivors of child-hood sexual abuse live with an ingrained sense of shame, even though they really did nothing wrong. Often, it's how adults reacted to the disclosure of the child that implants this shame. Parents and caretakers who turn victims away claim they are lying, or prioritize the abuser, making the child feel cast out and humiliated. Thus, relationships trigger these feelings of shame and humiliation because the emotional vulnerability that is needed for the relationship to grow puts them at risk of being rejected. Victims may see their abuser in their dating partners, which can taint potentially positive situations negatively. To this day, I still have to listen to my fears, because I sometimes think that the anxiety comes from a decision made by my spouse. More and more, at the very beginning of this discomfort, I practice the anchoring technique.

Once I recognized these issues in me, I knew something had to change. I'd never get the fulfillment in life that I wanted if I didn't address my social life. In fact, I put my emotional healing first over my financial hardships, but my uncontrollable emotions were the root of all my problems.

To heal emotionally and improve my interpersonal relationships, I tried many things.

First, I knew I needed to get used to social situations outside of bar-hop-ping, dancing, and drinking. I had to find a community where I could feel a sense of belonging, and where people from different walks of life could feel a sense of connection. So I joined an anonymous fraternity. I now understand just how beneficial it was for me at that time. It helped me survive. It forced me to be present with other people. Whereas normally I'd either be shielding myself behind alcohol or avoiding deep attachments or subjects, I now had to attend meetings and communicate with people. This fraternity activity allowed me to read books, share my experience with others, and share my feelings, my opinions. Speaking about myself was new to me. Repressing my emotions was so second nature to me since childhood, that it was necessary to consciously make the choice and the effort to express myself. I also had to take in others' ideas, experiences, and feelings, which helped me too. It taught me to live with others while sober.

At the end of the day, I don't think I could have changed my way of thinking and become more tolerant of others' suffering without the anonymous fraternities I joined. It helped dissolve my previous habit of judging others in similar or worse positions than me, opening up my ability to be empathetic and forgiving. All of this culminated in forgiving myself.

Therefore, I would recommend that the first step of healing is finding a safe environment to practice interpersonal communication. If you are a victim of childhood sexual abuse, you may feel blocked verbally. You have so much inside of you that you've been hiding for years. You never learned the skills you need to have healthy relationships or even healthy modes of communication with others. For so long, your main priority was to protect yourself, and that came first before enjoying harmless conversations, much less profound talks. If you can find an environment that can safely prompt you to build your interpersonal skills and practice communicating what you think, it can unlock your silence.

5

TRAUMA TAKES ITS TOLL

Trauma can affect more than just your emotional state and behavior. Due to the consequences, victims can struggle financially and educationally without knowing why.

Because of my second traumatic experience with my aunt's doctoral student, I associated negative emotions with high education. I essentially had a fear of pursuing further education, and I had an irrational distrust of college students. However, if I wanted to evolve in my career and job opportunities, I had to seek a better education.

When I finally went to college, I underwent a three-year computer programming program, as per the French college system. It was incredibly difficult for me, as my self-esteem was at an all-time low. It prevented me from finding a job in programming, as I was unable to showcase myself. After a few years of scraping by and holding jobs without much interest, I decided to enroll in a university in order to improve my computer skills. I was a bit older than the other students, which made me feel like I missed out on a lot. Even though I knew age shouldn't be a limit to education. However, I felt a deep sense of inadequacy, like I was far behind the rest of the people in my classes. Even if I tried my best, I felt like my work wasn't enough. Everyone else was better, smarter, and harder working than I was. In essence, I had a severe inferiority complex.

An inferiority complex is a common feeling among survivors of childhood sexual abuse. According to psychologist Alfred Adler, not everyone had a similar drive or self-belief to meet certain goals, and that might be due to a sense of inferiority. We all feel a little inferior, or not good enough, from time to time. However, certain people, particularly those who have undergone difficult childhoods, may live with an innate sense of inferiority that affects all areas of life. In other words, it's chronic low self-esteem that requires intense inner work to overcome. Otherwise, it can make a person feel unable to meet even their bare minimum goals in life, even if people external to them perceive them as able.

That's where I was. Even if I potentially had the ability to take advantage of my studies and my professional life, I couldn't help but believe that it wasn't possible for me. It was an uncontrollable surrender. Thus, it became a self-fulfilling prophecy, in which my lack of belief in myself prevented me from achieving anything. After only one semester, I left my university studies.

In hindsight, I recognize now that my university experience was bringing up blocked emotions from the abuse I suffered from the doctorate student. Going to my classes was that much harder because of the current discomfort running through me. I was demolished without knowing it. I consulted a guidance counselor at the institution, and I couldn't stop crying during the entire meeting.

While there were job fields that were lucrative, they didn't mean enough to me to actually accept working in them and be motivated to find a related job. I jumped from job to job, just trying to pay the bills and survive. I was unemployed for many periods of time. Consequently, I found myself moving in with roommates, barely able to pay my own bills. I was afraid I'd never achieve personal success and independence, afraid I'd be in poverty for the rest of my life.

I couldn't seem to find a job. It wasn't just about enjoyment, it was about lack of motivation. I struggled with my sense of identity, with my wants and aspirations. During that time, I genuinely had no clue what I wanted to be in life. What did I want to do? What did I want to give or produce in my lifetime? The indecision and aimlessness were frustrating to me.

All I could feel was anger. I was angry at everything; at workplaces for various things, at coworkers, at bosses. I was angry that the economy sucked, those jobs made life unenjoyable. I was angry that I had to work a job I disliked in order to survive. I blamed everything from society to every individual person who bothered me on a daily basis. I blamed my childhood. I blamed my family for not giving me the resources I needed. While I grew up in a middle-class household, the distance between us and the addition of my stepmother made it hard to seek or accept help. I couldn't trust anyone else with my life or future. I had to do everything myself.

As it turned out, I couldn't trust myself either.

Childhood abuse, emotional, physical, or sexual, can wither trust down to nothing.

For a society to continue moving along, trust between the individual units is necessary. A boss must trust the workers to take care of their responsibilities, and workers must trust the boss to give them their rightful rewards. Coworkers must trust each other to work efficiently and collaboratively. Customers trust the workers to complete their job effectively, and workers trust customers to pay what is owed. It's a system that would never work without a little bit of risk involved.

Unfortunately, survivors of childhood sexual abuse learn that risk is dangerous. It's not worth it. Because the one time they decided to trust an adult, an adult who is supposed to be knowledgeable, responsible, and take care of things, everything changed. Their trust was completely betrayed. The risk they took resulted in an immense loss of their mind, body, and soul. This betrayal can bring their healthy development to a halt. They learn that taking no risk and trusting no one, is better than trying or putting faith in others. As time will tell, this mentality can also be disastrous. It forces a person to rely only on themselves.

My childhood taught me to trust only myself. Unfortunately, that meant it was me against the world. I was projecting my distrust and trauma on everyone else, including my work. In reality, it was me against me. No one else knows what I went through. They aren't responsible for the devastating loss I experienced in childhood, the loss of autonomy and trust, of control and power over my own body. Of course, I wasn't responsible for the acts that my abusers took out on me. But I wasn't that child anymore, nor was I in that situation anymore. My abusers were no longer in my life. While I would have wanted justice, it would not have changed the course of my career or my living situation. It would not have affected my trust issues or my behaviors. Those things were up to me.

The whole time I blamed others, I wasn't taking proper responsibility for myself or my life. I was avoiding the problem and giving myself excuses for why I couldn't succeed and get the life I wanted. Doing this allowed me to continue escaping my pain. At some point, I had to stop living in the past and be more conscious of how I was acting and how my actions were leading to my perceived failure. Heck, even the shame and low self-esteem

I had were things I had to make peace with because a healthy mind would not engage in those emotions either.

I had to tackle those attitudes toward myself in order to undo the toll the trauma had taken on my life. First, I needed to overcome my emotional numbness

6

EMOTIONAL NUMBNESS

While rage marked many periods in my lifetime, others were marked by stretches of inner emptiness. I would feel blocked from my emotions to the point where I felt like I had to act out reactions and emotions to seem normal in front of other people. I thought I was broken.

Later in my life, I would realize this was a manifestation of disassociation, in the form of emotional numbness. A misconception is that people who have suffered severe trauma in childhood only deal with unstable emotions or emotional reactivity. While true, that's not the full story. The other side of the spectrum can also be a major force: feeling numb, empty, or disconnected from one's emotions.

Identifying and feeling certain emotions can be incredibly difficult for victims of sexual abuse. The experience is very individual. Some may even not understand emotions at all. For instance, I once met a woman who'd undergone a similar experience to me and who literally believed emotions to be cognitive or intellectual. In other words, she couldn't recognize her physiological response to emotions, only estimate what she should be feeling cognitively, by making mental statements, based on what she observed from life and movies. More often, emotional numbness feels like a disconnect from yourself and from reality. It's hard to really feel things when you have spent most of your life shoving those feelings down. If you have learned not to show or even experience your true feelings as a child, you will not be able to feel them, recognize them, or express them in a healthy manner as an adult.

How exactly does emotional numbness feel? It feels like being in a group of people, and someone announces positive news. Everyone is smiling, cheering, and congratulating. You recognize that they are happy for the person. You want to be happy for the person because you feel like you should because it's only right. You can cognitively make the decision that this is a good thing. However, you cannot seem to muster up a real, genuine expression of that happiness for them. It's not truly within you. Instead, you have to watch the others and act out their reactions, like a robot learning how humans work. This was me for a long time. I didn't know how to act. I had to mask myself in social situations and simply reflect on the external emotions of other people.

Many people describe this emotional numbness as a glass wall between them and the rest of the world. They are living, but they feel like perpetual observers looking in on everyone else living their lives. Others feel like their brain is muddled, and they are unable to extract from it a proper message to express outward. They know they feel something, but it's like a bad frequency on the radio, and they can't find the right channel. Otherwise, emotional numbness may also feel like zoning out from life, like your brain has taken a pause from the present moment. All of these factors can make it hard to have memories, to know yourself, or to trust yourself, decreasing overall self-esteem.

For me, naming real emotions was practically impossible. While I was going through something difficult, my nervous system would be in over-drive, and I had no way of receiving the message that my body was sending. I was in survival mode and emotions didn't matter there. I just had to get through it. Only when I was in the midst of fiery bouts of rage could I identify what I was feeling -- it was too powerful to ignore. Moreover, there is this interesting phenomenon in which anger is a more socially acceptable emotion than other forms of expression. Why is that? It all goes back to childhood conditioning.

Needless to say, chronic emotional numbness is not healthy. It is not strength, it is not resilience, it is not self-protective. It's a malfunction of the body's defense mechanism. Childhood sexual trauma can hack your nervous system. The long-term stress response can overheat your defenses, making stress hormones negatively affect the emotional center of the brain: the limbic system. High stress can surpass the levels of distress that your body and brain can handle, so everything just switches off. The stress meter breaks. No more emotions.

This sort of experience of high stress over a long period of time, coupled with an inability to properly manage that stress, can really fatigue the body. This can lead to brain fog, cognitive issues, memory problems, inflammation, and chronic fatigue, among other health problems. If you are experiencing chronic emotional numbness, you have been just barely surviving for a long time, and you must address this immediately. Without connecting to your emotions, self-love is impossible. Knowing what you want in life is impossible. Setting boundaries in relationships and expressing your needs is impossible. How can you even know your needs and desires? How do you know if you are doing something to please another person or doing something for yourself? How can you figure out your ambitions in your education or career, and grow the motivation to reach your goals?

Many of my life's problems could be attributed to my emotional dissociation.

One of the best things that the women's support group taught me was that victims do not have access to emotions. The reason for this is that we, as children, were not believed. It is a known fact in the field of child development that children learn everything through modeling their parents. Healthy parenting requires that the parent affirms and validates the child's sense of self, including their emotions. After all, emotions are involved in the process of memory formation: strong memories are tied with strong emotions, it's like a signal that tells the brain what is important to remember.

First, validation looks like accepting the child's emotions and allowing them to express them. Often, children aren't looking for a quick solution or feeling better. At their core, all they want is comfort, for someone to nurture them no matter how they feel, and make them feel listened to and acknowledged. When someone's emotions are regarded seriously, it feels like a sort of proof of their right to live as a person. We're on this earth to experience and feel, and if no one cares about our feelings, it's almost like a rejection of our existence.

More frequently, what happens is that parents aren't equipped to validate their child. Maybe they never learn to regulate their emotions themselves, or they believe emotions are not to be expressed. Some parents don't feel comfortable showing feelings or comforting their children. Other parents might just not get their children at all. For the most part, though, children's emotional needs are not seen as important because adults assume when the children grow up, their childhood experiences will be forgotten. Whatever the reason, parents will instead minimize the child's emotion, ignore it, redirect the attention to themselves (i.e. "This is nothing! When I was your age..."), or lash out in frustration.

What happens when the parent doesn't validate their child's emotions? Children will be unable to manage their own emotions, or at times even understand them. Some learn to repress their emotions because they have learned that it doesn't matter how they feel. This repression in itself can lead to a laundry list of negative consequences and health problems later in life. Repression is a form of nervous system dysregulation, and that can wreak havoc on the body. Other children learn only how to express emotions the way their parents express them, usually through fits of anger or avoidance. Moreover, they don't learn how to offer emotional comfort themselves. They may treat other loved ones based on how their parents handled them when young.

Overall, this consistent childhood emotional invalidation leads to an inability to express sadness, shame, guilt, and other difficult emotions in a healthy manner. This can lead to a general feeling of emotional numbness throughout life. Even if you have emotions, you repress them. It's impossible to connect with them, much less show them. Many survivors of childhood sexual abuse have a lot of pent-up sorrow and shame that were forced to push down. That's because they may have gone to a parent or adult who invalidates them, made them seem stupid or crazy, and pretended their experience didn't exist. Such children have no choice but to internalize this message and continue through life pretending as though their trauma doesn't exist, literally. Our brain during childhood is raw, underdeveloped, and made up mostly of the limbic system, which consists of the desires and motivations needed to carry out the most basic (but most crucial) human functions, like hunger, pain, pleasure, and all emotions. Because we don't develop highly advanced modes of conscious thought and processing until later in life, everything we learn during our younger years (before our teenage years) is unconsciously driven. And what we internalize or learn unconsciously becomes a stronger force than our conscious mind. So even if we know what we consciously want now as adults, it's difficult to override the habitual programs we picked up decades ago.

Unfortunately, emotional dissociation means much more than just disconnection from your emotions and sense of self. On a daily basis, you feel an untapped orb of negative emotion inside you that is not reflective of your current situation. It's like all the repressed emotion remains stuck in your body, coming out at inconvenient times, and causing you to fade away mentally from the moment.

For example, I remember one time I was driving around with a friend. We were talking about nothing and everything all at once; it was one of those rare moments of interpersonal connection that you wish would last forever. It was a long drive into the city for a medical appointment. We neared a highway, beside which sat a construction site. The loud noises of construction disrupted us. Suddenly, my friend turns to me and asks, "Would you ever want to live in the city with all this noise?"

I don't know why the seemingly innocent question prompted a sudden shift in my energy. All I knew is that I knew the answer to the question, I knew it would not be an affirmative response, and yet I couldn't bring myself to answer. For some reason, answering the question honestly made some part of me uncomfortable. Now, I might guess and say it was because of how specific it was to me, and how it forced me to provide a personal opinion. Providing my actual opinions and true feelings has always been a struggle for me. Sometimes I know the answer, but the question strikes me as too loaded and relevant to my personal bad experiences that I don't want to answer at all. Other times, I don't know the answer, or it's too complicated to answer promptly, and the fact that I need to gather my thoughts makes me freeze. I never learned how to organize my thoughts and opinions enough to speak my truth; instead, I would just go with the flow, avoid the uncomfortable, and let others lead the way.

Regardless of why the question made me lose my grasp of the conversation, it goes to show how dissociation cannot be predicted. Sometimes something so harmless can trigger it suddenly. After that question about living in the city, I could no longer properly express myself or verbalize my thoughts. A layer of anxiety bubbled beneath the surface of my mind, without any rational reason. That feeling of discomfort stayed with me, and I didn't understand it, nor could I get back to the present moment. That's what dissociation does: it leaves you stuck in an in-between state, unsure of how to proceed with life without letting an emotion pass through your body (as it should), and lacking the tools to process that emotion.

According to the fifth edition of the Diagnostic and Statistical Manual of Mental Disorders, dissociation is a "disruption" from the "subjective integration of behavior, memory, identity, consciousness, emotion, perception, body representation, and motor control." In other words, it is when you become disconnected from your physical senses, body, and identity. Everything you sense is reduced in power like there is a fog between you and the outer world. Dissociation manifests in a variety of ways, but it is generally an uncontrollable form of avoiding difficult situations or feelings, usually due to depression, anxiety, panic disorders, or any trauma-related disorder.

Because disassociation is a spectrum that varies from person to person, there are many signs that can point to it occurring:

- Tuning out of conversations

- Being dazed

- Staring off into space

- Slow response or reaction time

- Feeling unreal or the world feels unreal

- Feeling like an observer

- Social withdrawal in public

- Fogginess

- Moving or living on auto-mode

- Flat affect (no emotion, or emotional numbness)

- Forgetfulness

- Rapid mood swings

- Behavioral changes

Mild types of dissociation include daydreaming and spacing out. Anyone can "dissociate" at any time by getting lost in the events of a book. More severe types of dissociation can range from depersonalization to dissociative amnesia. Some people with traumatic histories may deal with a mixture of these at once, or have a specific dissociative disorder, such as depersonalization disorder or dissociative identity disorder. Regardless of type, dissociation can make functioning throughout daily activities a challenge.

A greater sign that you deal with dissociation is the feeling that your life is divided into two parts, in which your identity changes. Before a past event, you felt like a completely different person than you do now. In this way, dissociation has a major impact on your perception of your identity. You can feel detached from your past self, or you may feel like a different person from week to week. If your perception and identity are altered day to day, depending on stressful triggers, it can obviously be hard to maintain a stable sense of self.

Dissociation has its purpose, of course. It steps in when your stress level surpasses your perceived ability to cope with stress. Everyone has a stress threshold, or a limit, to where they can healthily and resiliently handle a difficult situation. Adults with a history of childhood abuse, physical, emotional, or sexual, have not been equipped with the emotional resilience tools to safely handle high stress. Even worse, for those with Complex PTSD, random triggers can make them feel like they are in a situation that they cannot cope with because it subconsciously reminds them of their traumatic childhood or a time in which they were helpless.

There is also another important factor: the perceived ability to cope with stress. We think that our abilities and limitations exist without our control. However, sometimes how we *perceive* our abilities and limitations can also impact our stress response. For example, if you are dealing with a stressful work deadline, how you perceive your ability to cope with the situation is what actually affects how you will cope. Do you believe you can handle it? What do you think is your "last straw?" Do you see yourself as resilient and capable? I am not saying, "If you believe you can, you can." That's too simple. Rather, it has been shown that a person's belief in their coping ability (self-efficacy in relation to stress management), can increase their limit to handle stress. That's bad news for survivors of childhood abuse because no one has ever taught them to believe in their ability to handle *anything* in life, much less any negative emotion.

Let's talk about the consequences of dissociative behavior. The effects of dissociation are worse than their actual occurrence. Instances of dissociating in the middle of conversation or situations have led to endless conflict and bickering with others. I have holes in my short-term memory that have made other people wonder if I am ever listening or if I even care about them. It has affected my perception of things and even my identity.

It is also what contributed to my moments of rage. After my dissociation resulted in issues between me and others, I feel guilty and responsible for not being in better control of myself. I feel ashamed for having the problem, a problem with a cause I don't even comprehend. Because I don't know why dissociative episodes are happening, I have no way of alleviating my emotional distress, so I can only escape the way I know how: anger. I have lashed out in anger at many people because of my dissociative tendencies because, at the moment, I had no other response or explanation to provide. It was like a way to protect myself because it was like a recurrence of the rejection I faced as a child, when I went to my mother with my emotions, and she turned me away.

I have learned now that victims of childhood abuse tend to experience much anger and a sensitivity to rejection as well.

Unfortunately, when you feel really foggy when it comes to emotions, reality can elude you. Not only at the moment but also later on, when you think back to your past day, week, or month. Your memories and life can feel washed out.

Even connections with people feel watered-down and shallow. You struggle to feel closer to people because you are not on their level of feeling. You can't rejoice for others in their happiness, nor can you truly feel sadness for them. It's very hard to feel empathetic when you can't even connect with your own emotions. That's how my experience was. I could only connect with others who were also "escaping" reality through alcohol or sex.

Participating in the women's support group helped me to overcome my emotional struggles.

Talking with the other survivors allowed me to process my emotions. We all went through similar experiences, so sharing them allowed me to reconnect with my own emotions in a controlled environment. Surrounded by other victims of childhood abuse, I felt safe being open. Even though it was difficult at first, the patient and calm setting allowed me to let down my defenses. It also allowed my true desires to shine through and motivated me. It further increased my need to know the reasons for my emotional instability, my inexplicable anger, my stomach aches, and my anxiety.

This brings me to the next step that I learned from my own experience: healing requires a desire, an obsession to want to heal and understand yourself. I could have easily gone on, emotionally numb and helpless, thinking that is how it's going to be forever. However, I was sick and tired of living like that. It got to the point where the pain of staying this way was more than the pain I would need to undergo in order to change. The prospect of continuing to live the way I was sounded more terrifying than staying the same. As I said, it's hard to get to a place where you have strong goals or aspirations when you are a survivor of abuse. Being in survival mode limits your optimism and perspective of life. That's why it's important to identify your main problems to tackle and find a safety net that can push you to the next level, like a supportive therapy group.

Once that desire sparked within me, I wasn't able to verbalize my emotions more. That meant I had to go on to the next necessary step in my healing journey: Identifying my emotions and growing self-knowledge.

Identifying and naming your emotions is a key grounding tool to confront dissociation. It is what can help release the emotions stuck inside of you for so long, and help you be more in-tune with your sense of self. After all, you can't improve a problem you don't know. Once you know what emotion you are having, you can be able to express it and address it. The women's support group gave us a lot of practice with the emotions that exist and how they feel in the body. Many therapy services offer information on emotions and the physiological responses that come with them, but there is also so much knowledge online. Learning about emotions and why they arise reduces our fear of them. That's why we avoid them, right? Because we don't know what or why such emotions are coming up.

Basically, I had to practice associating what my body was feeling with my emotion. So if I felt uncomfortable, which would usually be a signal or a trigger for dissociation, I had to lean into it rather than resist it. Anytime I felt low, down, anxious, or angry, I wouldn't push it away. I welcomed it as an opportunity to understand myself better. To do this, I had to get used to being more present in my body.

Over time, understanding my emotions led to greater self-knowledge. I got acquainted with my triggers and tried to reflect on where they came from. As I noticed patterns within myself, my trust in my own intuition grew. This is the value of self-knowledge: it increases our self-esteem because we know what we are capable of. It jumpstarts a domino effect where more self-esteem improves how we feel about ourselves in other areas of life. Another benefit of understanding my emotions is that I was getting better at validating myself. With all the positive benefits that my childhood stole from me, I was slowly but gradually giving to myself. Surely, I was on a positive trajectory in my journey of healing.

Finally, the plus side of understanding dissociation is that it gave me an awareness of how and why I have had the issues I've had. That simple awareness has given me more control when living my life. It has allowed me to reflect on my abilities. I sat and asked myself, "Okay, how much stress *can* I handle? Can I increase my limit every time?" It became a game of seeing how much of life's struggle, both small and big, I could withstand.

Overall, improving my emotional health was one of the keys to getting the answers to my past that I so needed.

7

Make a Difference with Your Review

Unlock the Power of Healing

"Kindness is the key that unlocks the
door of healing." - Unknown

Hey there, fantastic friend! Do you know how important it is to heal from
the past and build solid and loving relationships? Let me share a bit of my
journey with you.

Growing up, life wasn't easy. Childhood trauma cast a long shadow
over my life, making it hard to trust and connect with others. But I've
learned that healing is possible, and it starts with sharing our stories and
supporting each other.

That's where you come in. By leaving a review for *Healing Childhood Trauma* by Nancy Loyat, you can help others like us find the hope and healing they deserve.

Your review is a gift that costs nothing but a moment of your time. Yet, it could change someone else's life forever. Your words could help...

...one more survivor finds the strength to heal.

...one more heart mend from past pain.

...one more soul connected with understanding and empathy.

...one more dream of a brighter future come true.

So, will you join me in spreading kindness and healing? Leaving a review and making a real difference only takes a minute.

I highly recommend the seven-day challenge before you rate the book. The challenge involves practicing the grounding technique thrice daily for seven days. You will experience what it feels like to be grounded in the present, a fantastic feeling that can be obtained whenever needed. I created a short document that can be your guideline, but you can do as you please. Scan the following code to download it:

Once you have completed the challenge, scan the following QR-Code below to leave your review:

If you feel good about helping someone you've never met, you're my kind of person. Welcome to our circle of kindness and support. You're one of us.

I can't wait to continue this journey of healing and growth with you. Together, we can achieve so much more than we ever thought possible.

Thank you from the bottom of my heart for your support. Let's keep spreading love and healing, one review at a time.

With gratitude,

Your friend and fellow traveler on the path to healing, Nancy Loyat

PS - Did you know that sharing something valuable with others makes you even more worthwhile? If you believe this book can help someone, please pass it along. Let's pay it forward and spread the healing!

You can reach me at nancyloyat3@gmail.com

8

REMEMBERING

Remembering, when it comes to severe trauma, does not happen all at once. Rather, it feels like the pieces of a puzzle, one by one over the span of several years. Each puzzle piece might be a piece of information brought to the forefront of your mind by a trigger. It might be a mental image, intrusive thought, or a physical sensation.

When triggered, your body senses a certain aspect that reminds it of the time of the traumatic event. Triggers speak to your memory because the brain associates the messages of your senses with your memory. So even if you don't cognitively remember something, your brain still picks up and categorizes sensory memories.

The problem is when triggers occur during your day-to-day life, unexpectedly. When you can't predict when they happen, it's hard to have a handle on your reaction. It can be very disruptive to your daily life, leading to issues with friends or at work. For some, severe triggers can lead to panic attacks, which can make it difficult to function.

On the plus side, your triggers give you messages that you need to decode to further your healing. If you are unaware of this, becoming triggered can be a scary, dysfunctional thing that can lead to further fear, especially if you don't understand why they happen. For instance, my triggers led to dissociative episodes, which caused a lot of problems in my life. For other people, triggers can lead to severe anxiety and panic attacks that can make them avoid certain situations in life. The reason why getting triggered can be so limiting is that it can cause flashbacks, a panicked feeling of powerlessness, generalized anxiety, and even tactile sensations across their senses that feel as though the trauma is occurring again. All of these symptoms can make everyday life distressing, making it hard to concentrate.

I am sure I have gotten triggered many times, long before I even understood what was going on, considering how much of an impact dissociation had on my life. The thing about getting triggered is that the more you uncover, the stronger or more distressing such episodes can become. On one hand, this means you are peeling back the layers of your healing journey. On the other hand, it can also make things more terrifying, but I had the national victim assistance number handy, in case I felt the need.

Triggers are physical or sensory reminders that basically press the button in your subconscious brain and allow those painful memories to be dredged up. It's a flash that can activate a stress response. They are created out of our senses during memory formation. Even if we don't have the image in our mind of the memory, the sensory information is still stored, as well as the powerful emotions we felt at the time. Later in life, experiencing those sensory triggers leads to our brain turning on the alarm because it is afraid the same thing might happen. For instance, veterans with PTSD may be triggered by hearing gunshots or loud noises. Or a person who experienced physical abuse as a child might be triggered by the sound of a belt. Two people may experience trauma and triggers very differently, even if the event or situation was similar. This can depend on a lot of things, from personality to emotional intelligence, specific to the trauma and to the personal significance of the trauma to the individual. How powerful a trigger is to someone who experienced a similar trauma says nothing of their "strength" or "weakness" because there are too many factors involved.

When triggered, you basically sense a lot of emotions that make up for the sexual abuse. All you have are the residual feelings left over. In return, you forget an event that tainted your whole life.

When I was only five years old, a priest abused me.

When I became an adult, the memory bloomed into my mind while I was on a trip to the grocery store. I was in my car, waiting for the traffic light to turn green. Then, a flash. I had a visceral experience of sperm spraying into my face. It's hard to explain how you know what something feels like so vividly when you've never consciously experienced it before in your adult life.

I had finally received the last piece of the puzzle. I finally remembered the traumatic incident with the priest. My body began to shake uncontrollably.

The shaking scared me, but according to psychologists, this shaking is a normal trauma response. It is a form of therapeutic tremors caused by the limbic system (the emotional part of the brain) when it senses danger. Quite literally, the trigger set off my nervous system, leading to the body showing proof of this.

I was so shaken that I had to park my car. My hands shook, and I was no longer in the mental state to go grocery shopping. I called the national support line, a resource that helped me get on my feet, so to speak, enough to continue the day's errands.

In PTSD, re-experiencing those memories is common. Flashbacks can feel so real, that they eclipse the reality of the present moment. You literally feel like you are back in time, feeling the physical sensations of the memory. It's a bit terrifying, and you can feel crazy about it. Others may re-experience their trauma as intrusive thoughts and images that, while they aren't a full-body experience, are very disturbing and distracting.

While horrifying, the sudden memory was proof. Finally, I had confirmation of the events, which - even though I knew deep down that I had undergone them - still remained fuzzy because I couldn't believe in myself. No one else would have believed me. My mother didn't. So how could I? Now, though, that flashback was solid, on a full-body level, and I could almost feel myself back in that time.

The question is, why did it take so long for me to remember? It's all a part of the protective effort of the brain. When you are young, right after experiencing trauma, thinking about it or remembering can be so severe and overwhelming that the brain essentially keeps those memories hidden and off limits. Many people may forget or think they have moved on. But really, they never actually processed it.

Suddenly, later in life, those unprocessed emotions and memories will resurface. Does this mean you were never healed? Are you actually getting weaker or more vulnerable? Are you losing it? Are you losing your healing progress? No. Actually, it's just the opposite. Many expert therapists posit that when trauma memories resurface, it's because your brain senses that you are now mentally able to handle them. The memories and emotions that were once overwhelming and may have destroyed you, are now ready to be processed because you are ready. A deep part of you has now become stable, even if it doesn't feel like it. You are no longer living in survival mode. While it's still difficult, it actually means you are about to progress even further and finally heal those repressed parts of yourself the right way. It's almost like unlocking the highest level in a video game.

As horrifying as the sudden flashback was for me, it allowed me to feel peace and validation over my experience. This is because now I knew it to be true. Plus, being an adult who gained more respect and trust in me since childhood, I now could have faith in my memory.

I eventually reached out to my cousin, who had accompanied me to the priest's house. It turned out that, although she had no recollection of the event, she had been having terrible nightmares related to that day. To me, that was another confirmation. Even if it wasn't physical evidence one could show to the court of law, it gave me validation for my trauma. At the same time, it didn't mean I felt like I had "won." The only benefit I got from remembering was clarity; I was able to understand what had made me suffer so much and how it led to all the consequences in my life.

I knew that even though it felt like most of the problems in my life were caused by me, they actually resulted from something real and gruesome that happened when I was young. While doing my research, I read in a report on the impacts of sexual violence in childhood that the abuser is the one responsible for turning a person into a victim by way of their illegal and immoral act. Reading this resonated with me and changed how I saw myself. Previously, I felt like it was somehow my fault for "inviting" the abuse, that I had been doing something that other, innocent children were not doing to put me in that situation. As it turns out, this was a normal feeling that many survivors feel.

Then, when you finally realize that you are the victim, it still feels like a damning label. It's almost as if being a victim is something you chose to be.

You feel responsible for your own status as a victim. That's where the shame comes from.

So reading that gave power back to me because I realized that being a victim was not something I chose, it wasn't a part of my identity; it was something my abusers turned me into. I could finally hand over the responsibility for the acts to the abuser. It wasn't my fault, so I didn't have to be sorry or cry with shame anymore. While those feelings were valid, they no longer had a reason to exist. It's amazing how being aware of something or the reasoning behind something can free you from its power. Now that you know where it comes from, it loses its strength over you.

With this remembrance, I could feel myself progress further in my healing. I had to let those painful emotions wash over me in order to avoid further disassociation. Avoiding it would just set me back. Pushing it away would not help. The memory gave me long-needed answers that, while disturbing, would allow me to move forward. Like many says, the only way out of a painful experience is through. That's where the growth happens.

9

ANSWERS ABOUT MY PAIN

Everyone wants to know the truth, the what, the how, and the why. So much of our suffering can come from simply not understanding *why* we have the problems that we do. As many mental health experts say, awareness of the problem can free you from it. Obtaining awareness is often the first step to being able to solve your problem.

When it comes to a traumatic past, you have all of these mental health problems and challenges in functioning in daily life that you don't understand the source of. That can make things worse because then you start to wonder if you are the problem. Maybe you just need to try harder to discipline yourself. I've considered that possibility many times and did try a bit harder in my employment, my social circle, and in conducting myself in the way I desired. However, it never worked out, because my unconscious habits would take me back to point zero. I knew that I needed answers. I needed to understand why my life was the way it was, and why I felt the way I do. Only when I knew why could I figure out the solution.

The answers I got from the women's group would lead to me changing my life for good.

Let's go back for a second to that very first day.

I remember going up the stairs to the support group space. Outside the door hung a sign: *We believe you!* It was such a simple sign, a basic message. Anyone could tell it to you, and usually, it feels very superficial and fake, like a vague nicety. However, at that moment and in that context, in a place where people were supposed to understand the type of trauma I'd been through, the message was delivered. It was exactly what I needed to know. It gave me a sign that I was in the right place. And indeed, this feeling would grow as I went through the first few sessions.

From the very beginning, the group leader gave us clear instructions:

1) Do not give advice to others.

2) Let a person cry without intervening.

3) If you don't want to be touched by the other participants, say so, and the others will respect that right.

In other words, it created the perfect safe space we all needed to spill our sorrows.

We met every Friday morning, and we discussed a variety of topics. Prejudices about sexual assault were one of the first discussions we had, and it was a good ice-breaker. Everyone had a lot to say about the stereotypes that many people have about sexual assault. For example, there's a basic assumption that strangers are more likely to carry out sexual assault. As many survivors can attest, most abusers tend to be those closest to them or their family: relatives, neighbors, and friends. Another assumption is that victims bring the abuse on themselves, somehow. This is, of course, completely false, as young children have no capacity to even think about such horrid acts, nor would anyone of any age invite such a thing. Unfortunately, these stereotypes stop many victims from seeking help or justice. Even if a victim does speak out, some may claim that they are doing it for attention.

So many obstacles are in the way of a victim's path to healing from their suffering. Thus, victims internalize people's objections before they even try to seek help. In other words, they reject their own experience before others can. The ones who do try to talk to someone about their abuse face denial and gaslighting. So many survivors of childhood sexual abuse seem to have this in common with me: they told someone who denied their experience, telling them that their abuser would never do such a thing, and maybe it was just a dream. One participant in the group even mentioned that in her family, she was told: "If he has not penetrated you, it is not sexual abuse." I truly learned what it meant to minimize one's painful experience.

Eventually, we brought up the consequences of childhood sexual abuse. This fits in well with the denial aspect of parents because apparently, the trauma will have a greater negative impact on the child victim's psychological development if the parent denies the victim's admission of the abuse. Unfortunately, many parents or adults tend to brush the abuse away. They do this either by pretending it didn't happen or pretending that it won't have as big of a negative consequence on the victim.

Obviously, it is not the case that such parents are evil or bad. Many of them might just be in shock, horrified that something like that could happen. They remain in denial themselves, and out of their discomfort, they prefer to push the thought away. Denial is comfortable and less stressful. And because the children can't speak for themselves, it's easy to hide behind a fantasy.

The issue is that children, at a young age, are unable to see their parents in a negative light. It's very difficult to change your opinion on someone you look up to, who takes care of you, is supposed to love you unconditionally, has been sheltering you, and feeding you for most of your short life. As such, this creates a crisis in the child's mind. Instead of blaming their parents, they turn the negative emotions to themselves, creating that innate shame and guilt that remains throughout adulthood.

At this point, we were getting close to breaking the surface of the women's personal accounts.

The other women were all from different walks of life, all connected by our shared experience of trauma. It was baffling that despite our distinctions, our accounts were eerily similar, as were the effects that followed them into adulthood. Miraculously, dissociative symptoms were common amongst them, even if we did not realize what was happening. I wasn't the only one who struggled to stay in the present world. Many of them struggled with depression, health problems, with generalized anxiety. A lot struggled with relationships and that's why they were there; because their trauma was affecting their marriage or family ties.

Finally, we had to talk to the group about the circumstances of our abuse stories. Many of them were jarring, to say the least, with some having experienced continuous events of trauma throughout several years of their childhood. Others had their family members directly abusing them. While not all details were explained, the stories left unsaid still stuck with me.

When it was my turn, I felt the fear of being shot in the head by a sniper. The group leader told me this fear comes from the feeling that I was going to break the *omerta*, the law of silence upheld by the Italian mafia to keep members from giving up information if caught by the police. In other words, I was still maintaining the unsaid promise to my mother, without even trying. It was like her order for me to not tell my father or anyone else glued my mouth shut. For so long, silence had been normal for me, and that fear was the wall keeping me from speaking. I was helping keep the secrets that plagued me.

Essentially, I came to understand that I had been conditioned to keep my truth to myself. There were others reasons involved, of course. Survivors of childhood sexual assault keep silent because they have learned that no one will believe them. At some point, they may have even stopped believing in themselves. It's so easy for adults to disqualify a child's perspective. It's even worse when the child is now grown up; some people may be quick to assume that they remembered things wrong. In fact, this is why many victims never do try to take action against their abuser. Others may have tried to speak up but were shot down or ignored.

While I would have fear before discussing certain topics, I felt a sense of well-being surrounded by other women like me.

Getting an answer to that fear was like giving me the key to my freedom, allowing me to open the door whenever I wanted. Fear often comes from not knowing, but when you do know, you can be more in control of your response to that fear. I also came to understand better why I often became nauseous. That nausea was a warning from my child-self, who learned that speaking up is dangerous and pointless. It was the reason I sometimes would not even divulge seemingly normal details about myself or my opinions to others. I told myself to stay quiet before others would.

The group was just what I needed to finally break the silence. I felt safe and protected; the others were supportive, and I learned to be the same way. It became easier to sympathize and connect, especially since I realized many of their stories were just like mine. I felt close to them and understood them. Simultaneously, I felt understood. We discussed the little signs and things we had in common that others would not get. We talked about the sounds that irritated us, that triggered us, the words that brought back certain memories.

I learned to name my emotions and identify them at the moment. This helped me to no longer be overwhelmed all the time. I could be more in control of what was going on inside of me. Instead, I learned to welcome emotions, no matter how negative, without suffering. Finally, I could listen to myself. Because that's what's most important, isn't it? Listening to yourself and acknowledging your emotions first, even if other people do not.

One important emotion I had to acknowledge was my shame. Among psychologists who specialize in trauma, shame is one of the most destructive parts of being an individual who has undergone abuse, especially sexual abuse. Shame is a toxic form of guilt that goes beyond feeling sorry about what you have done. It is about feeling bad and regretful about *who you are*, even if it is not deserved. In other words, you have done nothing to feel shameful for, but you cannot help but feel at fault. Young children feel that if a parent or adult is angry at them or punishes them, it is because they failed to do something right. For example, I could have avoided going to the priest's house. If I hadn't gone, I wouldn't have put myself in that position. Or I should have asked the graduate student to take me home immediately. Or I should have been more quiet and listless so as not to attract the attention of my abusers.

However, all of these blameworthy things are irrational and unreasonable. It's like getting mad at a child for scraping a knee. Should he feel ashamed for having gone out in the first place?

First, it's important to note that these shameful feelings would not have come up if it hadn't been for adults not listening to me. The same goes for other victims of sexual abuse in childhood. When they go to an adult and that adult makes them feel like it is the child's fault or just does not believe them, it sends a message that the child has some responsibility in the matter. Children will feel that they were to blame because if they were innocent, their parents or the adult to whom they disclosed would have trusted them and gotten the abuser in trouble. Sometimes the parents get angry at the child's disclosure, and children, being unable to completely put themselves in other people's place, will attribute that anger as being about them. Because I was not allowed to talk due to the pain it caused my mother, I understood that when I spoke, my mother became sad. So I would not talk. Other parents may cause further damage by flat-out blaming the child for lying or putting themselves in a position that increases the risk of abuse.

Without this issue of disbelief or denial, the shame would not have a chance to grow into something larger and uglier than it should be. Shame should not exist in the first place, because the child is 100% innocent in such a situation. The law-abiding adult who chose to abuse the child is completely and absolutely to blame because they know the rules and should have complete control of their mental and physical faculties.

Let's talk about cases in which a child's disclosure does lead to action. While movies might show this as a heroic story of justice, real life is not the same. Often, a victim's family will turn away from them because of the disclosure. For instance, say a child discloses to a school counselor or social worker about an abuser who is a relative or family friend, which will lead to a series of legal actions that must be taken. Understandably, this can cause conflict within the family. Relatives may turn away from the victim, blaming them for disrupting the peace. It can lead to consequences like divorce or legal action taken against the abuser, which can cause resentment. Thus, such victims must continue to live in a tense environment during childhood since they still depend on their parents.

In either case, shame and guilt become a strong part of the victim's life. They feel disgusted at the act, at themselves, for not being "strong enough" to stop the abuse from happening. These negative emotions affect every facet of their self-concept, making them feel undeserving of love, good things, and happiness. They feel stripped of their dignity, innocence, and humanity. Even if positive things happen in their life, they may unconsciously avoid or reject them because it feels uncomfortable. They are not used to it. More likely is that they repeat their victimization, either by going through similar situations or enacting abuse on another, in some severe cases. Many victims end up chasing dangerous or toxic scenarios, not because they want to repeat the first abuse, but because they unconsciously want another chance to fix the problem. In other words, it's like losing a level in a game and playing it over and over until you defeat it. In life, however, the level cannot be won, it must be escaped. As for those who become abusive, they may seek to find their power in other ways by bullying other kids or picking up narcissistic traits for survival in adulthood. While this is not every survivor of childhood sexual abuse, it is a possibility.

Not only that, but these emotions of shame and guilt can be translated into anger and rage, especially later in life. As children, victims are unable to show their true anger and disgust at the abuser. This builds up inside them over time. Of course, it doesn't help that it can feel like everything and everyone is against you. You can be angry at your abuser, at your parents or family, at society, at the failing of the justice system, at yourself later in life, at the way that you can't get past it and live the way you want. Other things like difficulty in relationships, education, and work can also make you angrier at yourself. Moreover, if you struggle with showing healthy emotions like I did, you might express it as anger as well. All this anger mixes together and becomes explosive, irrational rage and no one seems to understand. It can feel like you are against the world.

In my experience, handing over the responsibility to the abuser without minimizing the harmful effects of the abuse was crucial to release some of the guilt and shame I held on to. I had to understand that I was not responsible for others' emotions by building boundaries.

It's important to create boundaries around your emotions. By boundaries, I mean you create a clear line between where you start and end and where others start and end in relation to you. Often, we who have suffered abuse may completely erase the lines or boundaries between ourselves and others, to the point where we don't know whose feelings we are feeling. Did we make a choice because we wanted to, or because we felt like it was the right decision to make someone else happy? In other words, we can minimize ourselves to such a degree, and maximize the importance of others. What this means is that our hypervigilant senses may pick up on people's body language and attribute every little sign as personal. We use that message to guide our own responses and actions in life. While to us, it may seem like a superpower, it's not. It's a broken detection system. We become incredibly sensitive to people's negative emotions, ignoring any positive emotions because we weren't trained to pick those up. Only negative emotions were important to observe to keep us out of danger. By recognizing that negative emotion from another person, whether it is obvious or not, we attribute it to ourselves. So if a coworker has a bad day, unrelated to you, and they come to work with all this negative body language, you may feel like it's your fault, or you did something wrong. Maybe you should have smiled more or spoken more nicely or helped with the tasks more. Then, you start to feel guilty and responsible for something that had nothing to do with you.

All this can be rooted back to taking responsibility for our trauma. For instance, when my mother denied my abuse, I internalized that as my fault. I felt guilty for making my mother feel like she was in a difficult situation. I felt responsible for the fact that she rejected my disclosure. This is called false responsibility, and it comes from the need to control other things as a child. Children are mostly powerless and try anything to feel like they can be in control. Some cry and have tantrums, while others try to appease their parents and do everything they can to be perfect and in control of whether adults will reward or punish them. Due to my family system, I must have learned to keep my emotions down in order to keep the peace, just as my mother wanted to keep my abuse a secret to maintain peace. If I could control my emotions and other people's responses, then there would be little problems. Unfortunately, this is not true in the real world. We cannot control anything outside ourselves. I cannot fulfill the needs of everyone around me.

Taking responsibility for only your own emotions and no one else's works both ways. Just as you cannot be held accountable for how another person feels, despite your actions (so long as you are not intending to cause someone hurt), others are not accountable for how you feel. This is important to remember when you are internally feeling resentful or blaming others. For instance, my issue was blaming everyone and everything around me for my circumstances. Anytime I felt angry, even if it had nothing to do with the person in front of me, I would think to myself, "Don't they see how I feel? Don't they care? Why are they making me feel angrier?" In this way, I was driving myself into a pit of victimhood. It was all about why is life doing this to me and why are they making me feel this way. In reality, many of the people in my life perhaps did not even know how I felt or even aimed to affect me deliberately.

Here's how I learned to name my emotions and some exercises you can do too:

Try an anchoring exercise that can help stabilize you in the midst of strong emotions. Anchoring refers to a technique in which you create an association between a stimulus or signal and an emotion, in this case, calm or peace. For me, the grounding exercise allows me to calm my anxiety, without having to structure my thinking. I do it without thinking, but taking the time it takes to calmly feel my unidentified emotion until I can name what is bothering me. To practice anchoring, you must repeat this many times before a situation arises in which you have to use it. Using this strategy will help you to change your fear in a second or even a fraction of a second. Then I can identify a fear (abandonment, rejection) and I can neutralize it, through anchoring, right now, right here. There becomes no need to argue or cause conflict. And this is where the miracle happens. I feel soothed and I no longer have to run away.

As a trauma survivor, learning self-regulation can be incredibly helpful for you. Self-regulation can help you deal with anxiety and fear when it is triggered in your daily life.

Anxiety is a common consequence of childhood trauma. The stress that a traumatic event puts a body through can manifest as a chronic anxiety disorder. Or the way that a victim copes with life following a trauma affects their risk for an anxiety disorder. After all, trauma can more often than not lead to PTSD, a severe anxiety disorder. However, many victims can also end up with social anxiety, panic disorder, agoraphobia (which is a fear of going out in public), and generalized anxiety disorder (GAD).

I have recently been diagnosed with generalized anxiety, and I am still affected by the consequences of childhood abuse. I have learned to live with this diagnosis now.

Joining the support group was one of the best things I ever did; it was a wonderful experience, and one of the most important steps in my life. I felt myself grow the most during that time.

10

TOOLS TO COUNTER DISSOCIATION

Remember when I said that dissociation for me felt like I lived a life split into two: before the trauma and after the trauma? Then, before remembering and after remembering. When I remembered, it felt like a piece of myself was coming back to me, or there was a seam in my mind that was re-sewn. This is because it alters your identity and perception of the world and your life. The more you can reduce the power of your dissociation, the more you feel like you have returned to yourself like you have a stable, stronger sense of self.

If you are struggling with dissociation, after fixing your substance abuse problems, the first thing to do in your life is to tackle it. That's what my life experience has taught me. Healing from dissociation helps solidify the fracture in your mind. Every time you experience a dissociative episode, there is a barrier separating you from your current experience of life. In that way, it causes distance between you and your relationships, your work, your desires, and your memories. For some people with severe dissociation, like those with Dissociative Identity Disorder (DID), there may literally be fractures in their mind created at the time of trauma. These fractures severely affect their identity to the point in which their brain creates more than one identity within them that switches when triggered. While that is a disorder that tends to be lifelong, dissociative episodes as a symptom can and should be improved to help you function better in life.

Finally, I will leave you with some key tools I learned to reduce dissociation. Grounding techniques are so important for people who have suffered childhood sexual abuse, as well as other trauma. The main issue with trauma and trauma-based disorders is that it is hard to stay in the present and live when the dark shadow of the past is always at the back of your mind, stopping you from properly enjoying the moment. To reduce this issue, grounding helps you focus more on the present and connect with what is happening in your current reality. It also helps distract from the difficult feelings of triggers.

In the self-help group, we had to exercise being more aware of when we dissociated. We did this by identifying the times when we dissociated ourselves from our bodies, and then took note of the circumstances of the event. For instance, if you are having a conversation with another, you must write down the times when you could no longer follow the discussion. The way to do that is to try to remember the last sentence right before the break in your memory. Often, this is what may have incited negative feelings from your past to rise up and trigger dissociation. The more you practice recalling the last thing you heard, the better you can train your memory to be. Then, you write that thing down and try to feel what emotion came up after that last sentence.

I had to take my notebook everywhere to put on paper what had just happened to me in real-time. One time that I did this, I had to explain to the friend to whom I was talking to why I was taking notes during our conversation. When I did, I suddenly felt guilty. Why did I feel guilty? I had no reason to feel that emotion in our exchange, which means that it came from the past, it was an emotion that had risen from my subconscious. When I reflected on the feeling in relation to what we'd been discussing, I found that something about the conversation triggered the remembrance of a word my mother had said to me when I told her about the abuse my uncle had done. As if I had been the cause of what happened to me. I think that stuck with me even without me knowing it, revealing itself as a deep shame within me.

This reflection led to another release within me.

Normally, the negative emotion would have led to me feeling defensive and lashing out somehow at whomever I was talking about. By being more aware, I avoided arguing with my friend for such a small reason that was coming from somewhere else, from my past. By identifying where it came from, I essentially diffused it.

As the experts say, awareness is the first step to change.

I was able to see the benefits of getting in touch with emotions from that instance, even with those with that I suffered the most. Because, for me, the real suffering is not knowing what's going on inside. When I ignore my emotions and cannot name them, I am only reacting to what is around me. I call this Hell because it is in this context that I express my explosive anger and I do not make friends. As I want to have harmonious relationships, make the best decisions for me, and stay in touch with my emotions, and then I get the most fantastic results. The world suddenly seems more pleasant and peaceful now.

Self-monitoring is one of the most important tools for dissociation and is derived from CBT. It's a skill that has to do with garnering awareness for your thoughts, emotions, and behaviors. Increasing your self-monitoring skills helps you better adapt and shift how you react to the situation. It branches off from mindfulness, which is a practice of focusing your awareness on the present moment without criticizing or judging it. That means you get in touch with the current situation and separate yourself from the subjective feelings. For example, if it is a usually stressful situation, you must distance yourself mentally and just observe the moment without any positive or negative emotions. You are just a witness. To practice mindfulness, and by extension, self-monitoring, you must focus your breathing and your sensory information, noticing how you feel physically, what sensations you experience, what you are seeing or smelling, and so on. Try to disconnect from your thoughts and instead, just watch your thoughts pass by with neutrality. This allows you to maintain clarity of mind and thus make better decisions and responses about the situation.

Mindfulness is very beneficial for reducing anxiety and depression, as well as improving your ability to concentrate and avoid zoning out. Many effective therapies use mindfulness in their practices, but you can do it at home. So, how can you begin implementing mindfulness? There are several techniques that you can add to your daily routine. For one, it's important to practice *deep breathing.* Slow, diaphragmatic breathing is when you breathe straight from your diaphragm, which is the area between your abdomen and your ribs. When breathing deeply, you will notice your stomach moving up and down. You should feel that the entire cavity expands upwards and outward. Deep breathing not only provides many positive health effects but also regulates your nervous system. It is doing the opposite of what your nervous system is forcing you to do in survival mode. Instead of breathing quickly and shallowly, having a higher heart rate and faster blood pressure, deep breathing makes your breathing pace slow, heart rate steady, and blood pressure decrease to normal levels.

For your mental health, deep breathing switches your brain's attention to the present moment. When you focus on your breathing, you come back to your body rather than remain zoned out. Dissociation is a trauma response to an elevated nervous system. When you pause the nervous system's alert, there is no longer any need for dissociation. Moreover, it grounds you to the present.

The focus on breathing is a reason why meditation is also an excellent tactic for grounding. Various types of meditation can help you improve your mindfulness in the short term and long term. The added bonus is that it provides mental relief as well. One meditation that helps me stop and get in touch with my body is the body scan meditation. With it, I get in touch with how my body is feeling. Being out of connection with our body can make us lose sight of sensations, hunger, and other key signs. For instance, you might feel anxiety physically, rather than mentally or emotionally, especially if you are not yet trained in identifying emotions. With the body scan meditation, you can see where your body feels tense if your digestive system is settled if your limbs are restless. With it, you will know that you need to take a break to rest or calm down. It's also useful for identifying key places in your body that hold a lot of trauma.

To do the body scan meditation, sit in a quiet place and breathe for a few moments until you feel centered. Then, start with the crown of your head, at the top, and focus your attention on how it feels. Is it light or tight? Tense or relaxed? When you're ready, move down to your forehead, face, ears, and neck, probing each area for any sensation. You are giving everybody part attention. Keep going until you have scanned the body all the way down to your feet. Doing this meditation regularly will improve focus, reduce long-term pain and tension, and of course manage your stress. More importantly, it's a way to check in daily to ensure you are not neglecting your body.

The following are some other meditations you can use to ground yourself and manage dissociation. The loving-kindness meditation can help you release resentment and practice love. There are several ways you can practice it, but in general, it requires getting into a relaxed space, taking deep breaths, and then visualizing yourself giving and receiving love. First, think about someone who you love and imagine you are sending love and kindness to them. Then, imagine someone else who loves you is washing over you with waves of love. Finally, visualize someone who you have difficulty loving, perhaps someone who hurt you (not your abuser). Rather, it should be someone with whom you have a difficult relationship. Imagine yourself sending love and kindness to them. The people you imagine do not have to be the same people every time. Often, this meditation can help if you are feeling alone, having relationship conflicts, or are resentful of someone in your life or your past. It helps you release that negative emotion and find peace. Moreover, you practice understanding what love feels like and feeling connected with other people.

Remember, these techniques don't always need a huge chunk of time to accomplish. All you need is enough time to go through the steps, and sometimes 5 or 10 minutes is enough.

Following meditation scripts on YouTube can be very helpful if you lose track of your thoughts during a solo meditation session.

11

THE 3 SHORT STEPS STRATEGY

THE GROUNDING TECHNIQUE

Learning to ground yourself is one of the most important tips I have learned. The goal of trauma healing is to make peace with your emotions. If you don't feel them, how can you make peace with them? If you can't make peace with them, the repressed emotions will come out in insidious ways that will wreak havoc in your life.

There is also a slew of other reasons to practice grounding yourself. For one, it helps you be more present with life so that you can actually live it and improve it. If you cannot be down to earth, it is hard to pay attention, to concentrate on the important stuff, be it at work or in your relationships, and it can make it difficult to reduce the power of triggers related to trauma. Grounding techniques help you restore peace and balance in your nervous system when you are mysteriously troubled out in the world. Over time, you will also get the added bonus of improved self-awareness and reflection to pinpoint your problem areas and reduce them.

One particular grounding technique has helped me so much. There are so many out there, but I would recommend choosing one to consistently practice. After enough time, you will begin to do it automatically.

Even four years after learning this grounding technique, I have been able to keep good relationships with my boyfriend, my co-workers, and the customers. I don't react to bad comments anymore. It has saved my life: I have kept my job, I like my colleagues, and I can communicate with family, without the old tension or any fear. It's unbelievable how effective it has been. It's as though my past no longer colors my present, which is so freeing.

Now, before I answer other people with something negative because I feel ignored or rejected, I do this grounding technique. It may seem easy or too simple at first, but it helped me gain trust in my emotions and make more conscious decisions.

Here's how to practice the technique:

First, sit (or stand) with your feet flat on the ground. If it helps, imagine your feet are rooted to the ground, so you can physically feel "grounded."

Second, look around you. Name 5 things that you see in front of you. Name 5 things that you hear. Then, name the emotion you feel at that moment.

For example: "I see a table, I see a chair, I see a plant, I see a door, I see a glass of water. I hear the clock ticking, a car passing by, and the sound of the refrigerator." (If you can only hear less than 5 things, that's okay). Then, calmly, try to listen to your emotions. If you can't identify any emotion, do the technique again. This time, name 4 things that you see and 4 things that you hear. Now, try to name the emotion you feel at the moment. Repeat as many times as you need in order to feel more in touch with your emotions, but each time name one less item (i.e. name 3 things you see and 3 things you hear, then name 2 things you see and 2 things you hear and then name 1 thing you see and 1 thing you hear).

It's possible that you can't identify the emotion. This is normal among people with severe dissociative symptoms, just like me. It may take some time to be able to feel or understand your emotions, but every time you try this technique, you can see your progress. The first time might take you four sets of the technique. After a couple of weeks, you might only need two sets.

If you can, I recommend doing this exercise three times a day, but one a day is fine. It helped me during high-stress situations when I was out and about in the world, in a waiting room, during the break at work, and even before clients reached my workspace. Luckily, practicing this technique daily will work your grounding muscle so that you are better able to take a pause, naturally, when you need to.

For my part, it took me *three days*, doing this exercise three times a day, to be able to name anger. I couldn't identify that I felt anger before I exploded. Now, the more emotions you learn to identify, the more levels of deep trauma-related emotions you can unlock from your mental prison. Remember that naming something reduces its power. Learning something reduces your fear of it. This grounding technique has helped me break free from discomfort and the urge to run away in the face of difficult emotions.

Moreover, this is a very good tool to use when you are overwhelmed by emotions and don't know how to act next. Instead of reacting according to your first impulse, you can stop and think about how you want to respond to the situation. This will allow you to have greater control of yourself, your actions, and your life.

12

THE 5 FREEDOMS

from Virginia Satir

The 5 Freedoms technique is aimed at helping you boost your self-esteem. The technique called The 5 Freedoms is to overcome stigma. It was created by psychotherapist Virginia Satir, who identified five things we must showcase in life and how we communicate with the external world. Satir's work aimed to help people "become more fully human," and to do that required an intimate knowledge of self and others.

Virginia Satir's 5 Freedoms is a set of affirmations that can help boost your self-love. It provides a set of five important reminders for us to break free from limits holding us back from true self-love and self-respect.

First, why is self-love so important? Self-love is something that feels beyond the reach of survivors of childhood sexual abuse. It's hard to feel worthy or valuable and thus, it's a bit difficult to value ourselves or put ourselves first. Sometimes, what can be most healing is the compassion you give yourself that no one gave to you growing up. There is a common idea that the root of negative emotions is an absence of love. When you feel anger, fear, anxiety, and other difficult emotions, they can be perpetuated by the fact that no one ever comforted you with those feelings in childhood. Feelings left invalidated will continue to resurface, and you have no way to comfort yourself because you don't know how. The solution may just be to fill up that space with love for yourself. Essentially, you are re-parenting yourself by addressing those negative emotions. You pretend to be the parents who didn't fulfill unconditional love towards you by loving yourself.

The problem is that it is hard to love yourself.

You might have negative self-beliefs that you picked up in childhood, which can make it hard to accept yourself. After all, how can you accept yourself when you don't like who you are or even (in some cases) know who you are?

To start loving yourself, you must begin by reducing your negative mental loops. The way that you talk to yourself in your mind affects how you feel. It can be hard to control your thoughts when you have never tried directing your focus inward. But the good news is that it is possible. With practice and repetition, you can absolutely guide your mind to think and believe better things that will actually support you. To do that, you must practice affirming the following five freedoms that you are entitled to. By affirming, I mean reminding yourself and repeating to yourself these new beliefs that will help you free yourself from your mental limitations.

The Freedom To Be

Simply being is a difficult thing to do. It goes against everything we've been conditioned to do. *Being* is about living as you naturally are without rejecting yourself. Remembering this freedom helps bring us back up to float above the dark depths of the ocean of the past, as we tend to be drowning in it. It also allows us to more fully embody ourselves and who we really are. We often can remain in a dreamlike state in which we continue to replay our history, or we may imagine fantasies about things we want and desperately desire, without coming back to earth to focus on our current life. When we choose to just be, we can better connect with our true selves and feel peace with the world. It also means being authentic and getting rid of our need to act a certain way to show an image to the world or to escape the shame of being ourselves.

To affirm your freedom to be, simply remind yourself daily, "I am free to be as I am. I am who I am. I don't need to do anything, I can just be." These statements aim to give you more peace if you are dealing with shame or anxiety at any given point. For instance, when I am feeling low about what I have accomplished, I instead remind myself that I am free to simply exist on this earth, and that I have as much right as anyone to live and enjoy life no matter my material accomplishments.

The Freedom To Decide What You Think and Feel

This freedom returns the power and free will back to us. Often, we can get caught up in keeping down our real thoughts. Sometimes most of our suffering comes from judging ourselves for our thoughts and emotions, or from rejecting them. As a result, we further disconnect from ourselves. We think there is always a way we should feel or think based on some random standard the world has generated.

However, these standards are irrelevant, or they may be subconsciously driven by you to protect yourself. Many survivors have an inner critical voice that sounds just like the adult or parent that once pushed them away. So your negative beliefs about yourself may not even actually be your own. Affirming this freedom gives you space from these negative, critical voices in your head. It gives you the ability to distance yourself from anything that isn't your decision. Then, you can really look at what you are actually believing and thinking inside. You can choose what you want to think or feel. If you want to accept how you are feeling, you can. If you would rather be thinking about something else, you can. The point is that it is your choice and no one else. More importantly, it's not an automatic response to life, but your decision.

For example, say that you do not get accepted to your dream job after applying and working so hard to get in. Of course, it's natural that you would feel bad. However, you want to make sure you are not feeling bad because you feel like you have to feel low, or because you feel some sort of a shame because you are thinking what your parents, family, or friends might think. Or you might take the news as a sign that you will never get your dream career or succeed in life, and you spiral into negative emotions that prevent you from trying to find another job. Instead, by affirming your freedom to decide how you think and feel, you can choose to only feel disappointed by the unfortunate news, yet know that you will be fine, and you can find better opportunities.

The Freedom To Feel

Many of us have not learned how to feel. Most of us learned how not to feel, and how to repress and avoid expressing our feelings. In this way, we continue to invalidate ourselves, just as people did when we were children. With the freedom to feel, you can experience your feelings as they are, without worrying about how you *should* be feeling. It's about being authentic and truthful to yourself when processing your emotions.

We never want to feel wrong about how we feel. If the situation calls for negative or low emotion, feeling bad on top of that can exacerbate it. Remember that having the freedom to choose how you feel is about consciously accepting that how you naturally feel is valid, without letting it consume you. It does not mean rejecting your emotions because you believe you shouldn't be feeling them in the first place. That is neurotic and leads to unprocessed emotions. Instead, give yourself time and space to feel your emotions as they arise.

The Freedom To Ask

It's so easy for us to avoid seeking help and asking someone for support. Sometimes we think we can't ask until we get the okay or permission. This can come out of insecurity or out of people-pleasing behavior. We don't want to make others feel inconvenienced. It's almost as if we have given away our will to ask and seek help or to choose what we want. It comes from a lack of self-respect.

This can be rooted back to a time when someone took away our right to choose to seek help. Or when we tried to raise our voice, but someone forced us to turn it off. We learned to keep our heads down, our voices small, and our needs turned off.

Independence is not about believing you are alone. It's about having confidence in yourself to know when you can take something on yourself and when to ask for help. It's an inner wisdom that allows you to just ask others when you don't know because you are not meant to know anything. Being too nervous or hesitant to seek the aid of someone we know or someone who might have good advice or support is a trauma response. Anyone with a healthy sense of self can do this without worrying about how the other person feels because it's their right.

The freedom to ask also goes for asking for what you want, be it love or other goals. It's the people who need love the most who often cannot ask for it in the right ways, if at all. I urge you to practice asking for it.

The Freedom To Take Risks

To live is to take risks. Leaving one's comfort zone can be so hard for traumatized individuals. Discomfort is dangerous because it may mean getting in trouble. Unfortunately, this stops us from progressing in life because we can't improve or grow if we don't take risks. It can stop us from taking action or making moves that could change our lives in a good way. We grew up fearing the risk rather than having faith in the possibility of good. Taking action is always the only way to shed our layer of victimhood. Actions take us into the future, and choosing what we do puts our future in our hands. We also can feel more responsible for our actions and the consequences, rather than feel like life is always happening to us.

Living according to these freedoms can sound difficult, but that's only because we have been in the prison of our minds for too long. When we can unlock the chains, we can feel the immense beauty of freedom. By freedom, I mean increased power in ourselves. Acknowledging that you do have the freedom to be, think, feel, ask, and take risks as a human helps you accept who you are and be more secure in communicating that.

Moreover, these freedoms try to go against the construction of perfectionism, which can be the most damaging lie we tell ourselves. There is no more perfect way to think or feel or be, other than as you are. Of course, you can choose how you want to experience life and react to it when you get to know more about yourself. That does not demand perfection. It asks for acceptance of yourself now and a willingness to gradually work on the things you can change. You don't have to erase how you feel now if you possibly want to be someone who feels differently in similar situations.

For example, let's say you no longer want to blow up when your partner comes home late because you panic and think they are cheating on you. Trying to do this perfectly from the get-go will not work, because you don't yet understand yourself. It will make things worse because now if you slip up, you will feel frustrated with yourself. Why can't you respond "normally?" The right way to do this is to accept that you can feel anxious about your partner cheating on you. It's a fair thing to feel. However, you can also mentally process your thoughts. You can say, "I have the freedom to feel and think whatever I feel or think. Yet, I also have the power to rationally understand that I don't know all the facts. I accept my emotions now, but I also know that emotions will pass." This is a form of self-regulation. You are being who you are without letting your emotions overtake you. Finally, you can remember that you have the freedom to ask for more love and support from your partner, to help you feel secure in the relationship and less anxious in the future.

As you can see, implementing the five freedoms in your life increases your mental discipline and emotional intelligence, while strengthening your ability to communicate.

13

CONCLUSION

Many times in my life, I thought I wouldn't be able to get through major obstacles. The secret I had kept for so long was the most defining moment of my childhood, and I still am displeased that it had to be such an unfortunate event. Being in a religious society that put respected adults above innocent, victimized children impacted me on an individual level.

Childhood sexual abuse is a dark secret that can be held by the community. Family, friends, and neighbors can be implicit in keeping this horrible act covered up. Worst of all is when your own parent denies your abuse. Unfortunately, this problem can be widespread when it comes to people who have a lot of power and control over a community. Be it religious figures, successful respected individuals, or people in high positions, sexual abuse can occur to those with the least amount of power: children.

Unfortunately, this powerlessness can continue to resonate in the victim's mind, even when they become adults. In adulthood, you are supposed to be free and independent, ready to make your own choices and choose your fate. Yet, the claws of trauma can lead to many negative consequences that keep such a person frozen in place, even in adulthood. They can be limited by a number of psychological symptoms, from depression to PTSD. They are more likely to be held back by an addiction or a dependence on unhealthy sexual relations.

To this day, I wonder how many other victims those abusers in my life left in their wake. How many other children did the priest invite into his home who didn't have the resources to seek justice? How many other young children did the graduate psychology student prey on after his research? It chills me how easily victims can be locked into silence, how easily these abusers, these criminals, can avoid responsibility.

At the end of the day, my healing falls into my hands. The same goes for all victims. While justice would be the best thing, it won't heal the many consequences of trauma. More than anything else, I had to work on my emotional numbness, so that I could at least use my emotions and feel like a human. Dissociation had taken away my connection to myself, and getting it back would be the greatest reward. Victims with dissociation are surviving, not living to their best potential. When I could learn the root of my dissociation, why I felt emotionally numb, and why I felt angry all the time, I could learn to be more aware of myself in daily life.

Other coping mechanisms can be a crutch that prevents you from developing. They may be protecting you, but at some point, that protection becomes more toxic and harmful. At some point, you need to choose the coping mechanism that will actually help you and let go of the ones holding you back. For me, it was sexual relations to avoid intimacy and using alcohol to numb myself and keep my traumatic memories at the back of my mind. I needed to cut myself off from these things in order to recover my memories, find answers about my trauma, and finally heal.

While I tried many fraternities to gain more experience expressing myself to people and other therapies, I found the most peace with the women's support group geared toward childhood sexual abuse survivors. If there is one takeaway you can get from reading my account, it is that finding a therapy group similar to your situation is so beneficial to feeling less alone and more understood. Many survivors of childhood sexual abuse experience similar effects and consequences in adulthood, while general support groups might not feel so accepting.

Some of the techniques that helped me the most are summarized here:

1. Learning to name emotions: Know what the many emotions are and how they may present themselves in your body so that you can be more aware of them.

2. Anchor yourself in times of high emotion using a mantra, a mental image, a movement, or an object. For example, use a bracelet that will bring you ease when you are feeling overwhelmed.

3. Counter dissociation with the following tools:

4. Deep breathing to settle the nervous system

5. Mindfulness

6. Body scan meditation

7. Loving-kindness meditation

8. Grounding Technique

9. Name 5 things you see and hear, then identify how you are feeling. If you can't name the feeling, then name 4 things you see and hear, then 3, then 2, then 1, until you are able to connect with your emotion.

10. The 5 Freedoms: Remind yourself that you have the right to these five freedoms by affirming them every day.

11. The freedom to be

12. The freedom to choose how you think

13. The freedom to feel

14. The freedom to ask

15. The freedom to take risks

I know so many survivors of childhood sexual abuse can struggle to find the right information to get them started on their healing journey. Now that you have a head start on what you might need to do to make progress in your life and break free from the hold of your trauma, it's time to start. It's time to take responsibility for your healing, no matter what age you are. When I decided to stop playing by my unconscious trauma response's rules and start figuring out why I was the way I was, I made major breakthroughs. It was what eventually allowed me to discover more of my trauma memories and understand my automatic behaviors.

Once you know the problem, you can solve it. In this book, I laid out significant moments of my life that shaped me, as well as moments that sped up the healing journey. I hope that you, whenever you are reading this, can use my example as a way to jump ahead. Perhaps you never considered that you might be suffering from dissociation. Perhaps you never thought about how you processed or regulated your emotions. Or maybe you thought a support group wouldn't help you. I hope that my account can help you have more clarity on what you need to do next if you have a similar situation.

Moreover, I recommend that everyone try the grounding techniques and self-love exercises I provided that have helped me the most. If you believe they can support you too, please get started on them immediately and add them to your daily routine. Act like they are a medication that will cure you if you take it consistently. Because, I promise you, the most healing comes from learning to recognize and manage your emotions and learning more about yourself through self-reflection.

Finally, I urge you to be more present in your life. This world is fleeting and as we traverse through love and loss, our pain can keep us stuck in the past and unable to fully enjoy the moment. Being more grounded and present will get you in touch with yourself, your loved ones, and the world. Then, you can truly move on.

14

RESOURCES

Rapport d'enquête AMTV mars 2015. (2015, March). Mémoire Traumatique. Retrieved July 14, 2022, from

Dealing with triggers. (n.d.). Opening the Circle. Retrieved September 19, 2022, from http://www.openingthecircle.ca/defining-abuse/dealing-with-triggers

The long-term effects of childhood sexual abuse : Counseling implications. (n.d.). American Counseling Association.

Claims, I. (2018, July 19). *Does Sexual Abuse in Childhood Impact Development and Intimacy in Relationships? [Video]. YouTube.* Retrieved September 19, 2022, from https://www.youtube.com/watch?v=Xo8eqgHxSV8&feature=youtu.be

Adult Manifestations of Childhood Sexual Abuse. (n.d.). *ACOG. Retrieved September 19, 2022, from https://www.acog.org/clinical/clinical-guidance/committee-opinion/articles/2011/08/adult-manifestations-of-childhood-sexual-abuse*

Long-Term effects of child sex abuse. (2021). *Abuse Lawsuit. Retrieved August 1, 2022, from https://www.abuselawsuit.com/resources/effects-of-sexual-abuse/*

Quiet Revolution. (n.d.). Retrieved September 19, 2022, from http://in dividual.utoronto.ca/hayes/xty_canada/quietrev.html

15

CHILDHOOD SEXUAL ABUSE RECOVERY WORKBOOK

HOW TO MAINTAIN RELATIONSHIPS AND BUILD TRUST

INTRODUCTION

I was expecting a return call from the women's sexual assault center. I was shaking, so afraid that I couldn't even sit still. The exact word for this is anxiety, but I didn't know what it was before the group sessions.

I know how it feels to nervously await the next steps in your recovery journey. You are not alone in this feeling of deep dread and anxiety. Often, figuring out how you will move forward and who you will confide in is the most challenging part of healing.

But I also know that support groups were essential for me. For over 22 years, I have found peace, healing, and salvation within Alcoholics Anonymous groups. I felt more comfortable there than anywhere else. I could finally talk freely about my problems living with others and the responsibilities I had always refused to take on.

Except that at the last meeting, I was falling apart without knowing why my body started to shake uncontrollably. The cup of coffee in my hand wobbled, nearly spilling over the rim. I began to feel physically sick and decided to leave before the end. It was only after the whole ordeal that I understood what was happening.

My past was catching up with me. An AA member at the meeting reminded me of my uncle, who sexually abused me. I then experienced bodily ailments identical to those I had felt in my childhood: the same pains when my mother had taken me to the hospital. The doctor didn't know what was wrong. It was these abdominal pains that reappeared at the AA meeting.

This is just one piece of my story, which might be completely different from yours, but that doesn't mean I am the only one. In the following chapters, I will share some exercises learned from the sessions held at the women's sexual assault recovery center. These are, in my opinion, the ones that have made me progress the most in healing.

But you may need to learn why these steps are essential in moving forward in life. I am here today to tell you that learning coping skills, eliminating triggers, and living a healed life means stepping into true happiness.

We will talk about survival modes, feeling your emotions, feel-good activities, and how you can work towards recovery. This workbook is a tool to put what is not yet possible to name on paper. I am here to share more healing practices, including de-victimization and building trust with your spouse.

All of it is in one place so you can live a fuller life and finally feel like yourself again. You will learn to develop close and beneficial relationships with friends and partners, reduce stress levels, step out of "fight or flight" mode, and reframe your mindset around this trauma.

17

VICTIMS' SURVIVAL MODES

What is Sexual Abuse?

Childhood sexual abuse never looks like one kind of action, it isn't always one kind of person, and it is never your fault. Many different behaviors are categorized as sexual abuse, and physical contact is not something that needs to happen for it to be considered as such.

An action doesn't need to be completed to be regarded as sexual abuse. Your trauma and experiences are valid, and you deserve to be heard and healed.

Denial and confusion are some of the most significant hurdles you will need to jump over in this journey to healing. But when you understand precisely what you have been through and how it may still affect you today, you can seek a helping hand.

The simple acknowledgment of your history of abuse is something that takes massive amounts of courage. However, healing is possible with enough time, the right healing tools, and support from the right people.

It is important to note that there are different kinds of childhood sexual abuse, some of which include (but are not limited to):

- Exposing oneself to a child online or in person.

- Incest.

- Exposing a child to sexual content or activity (again online or in-person).

- Sexual words and harassment toward a child (including calling a minor or messaging them with sexual intentions, phrases, or imagery).

- Rape.

- Prostitution or sex trafficking of a minor.

- Physical and sexual assault (including but not limited to intercourse, masturbation, sexual touching, or other sexual acts)

While the physical effects of childhood sexual abuse are prevalent, the psychological ones are just as important to face. Disassociation, or mentally checking out and blocking out memories of traumatic experiences, is highly common regarding childhood sexual abuse. This is due to painful memories, so the brain (to protect you) buries them deep. This means that if you have experienced having a hard time remembering childhood memories, some version of abuse may exist there.

Trauma and the Brain

In a time of crisis or chaos, where your physical body can't do much to protect you, your brain will enter "survival mode." This just means that your brain functions differently when you experience something stressful. Our brains don't assess situations before locking down and entering "fight, flight, freeze, or fawn" reactions.

Our brains can turn on and off certain areas like a light switch. When you experience external or perceived stress, your brain's "thinking" area will dim. At this point, your mind and body will simply react without analyzing situations. You may find yourself doing things you usually wouldn't or avoiding certain situations without meaning to.

Survival modes are subconscious ways of living and acting. They bubble to the surface when we experience something shocking and are our brain's protective method. Your survival modes were developed well to help you survive. They were your only protection and kept you through unbearable situations.

These immediate brain reactions were developed throughout your childhood. However, you could still be living in survival mode without knowing it. It was how you grew up; it was your "normal." But at some point. You don't need this protection anymore, even if your brain still acts this way.

In this chapter, we will work to identify your survival modes and understand the most common stress reactions. It's time to allow yourself to recognize when you are acting subconsciously, and your survival mode is leading the way.

Understanding "Fight, Flight, Freeze, and Fawn" Reactions

The most common categories that survival modes fall under our flight, fight, freeze, and fawn. Understanding these categories will help you gain clarity on how you've handled your experiences until this point in your life.

Understanding these categories will help you know how you've handled your experiences until this point in your life. These stress hormones that are released either cause you to flee the danger (flight), face it aggressively (fight), pause and hesitate (freeze), or appease the danger (fawn).

These are simple physical reactions caused by a trigger, meaning that you don't pause to think about your body's reaction; they just happen. Below are ways each stress response may manifest:

Fight:

This response happens when you are in danger, and your body concludes that you can overpower that danger in many ways. This can be seen as a clenched jaw, grinding your teeth, attacking the danger source, intense feelings of anger, stomping your feet, crying in anger, attacking yourself, or even a burning feeling in your stomach.

Flight:

The flight response occurs when your body recognizes that you cannot overpower the source of danger. Your body will experience an increase in adrenaline, which can help your body run away with greater stamina and longer than you usually could. Living in a flight survival mode, you may be seen as over-exercising, tense or trapped, fidgeting with your fingers or clothes, restless, racing heart, and darting eyes.

Freeze:

The freeze response happens when you experience stress, but your body doesn't react or move. This occurs when your brain tells your body that you cannot fight or run away. Signs you are experiencing the freeze response include a deep sense of dread, feeling stiff or numb, flushed or pale skin, heavy sweating, decreased heart rate, and legs that feel heavy.

Fawn:

The fawn response is much less common in daily life, but it happens when the fight, flight and freeze responses are unsuccessful in a current or past situation. The fawn stress response is most often seen in people who grew up in unsafe family environments. This stress reaction can be seen as excessive people-pleasing, over-agreement, constantly trying to be helpful, and your main concern is making others happy.

The fawn response is caused by multiple things, including overdependence on what others think of you, a great lack of boundaries, easily being manipulated, and codependent relationships.

The Consequences of Childhood Sexual Abuse

Childhood sexual abuse has been known to affect people well into adulthood, especially if it goes unattended or is blocked out. These traumatic experiences can lead to higher rates of depression, marriage and relationship hardships, intimacy troubles, and other areas of psychological distress.

While it may feel like everything is happening to you, this does not mean you are responsible for what has happened. Your brain has worked to protect you from being hurt in worse ways, and that is a fantastic thing. So do not blame yourself for simply finding ways to survive.

Living in survival mode is a consequence that many experiences after experiencing childhood sexual abuse, but you may also find yourself struggling with other consequences. This doesn't mean that healing methods you have tried in the past aren't working or that you are broken; it just means that you have survived the worst and will continue to fight until you have moved forward and healed.

In childhood, some signs you may have exhibited when you were younger likely still affect you today. These include developmental delays, self-isolation, behavioral problems, social difficulties, low levels of self-esteem, signs of dissociation, a hard time adjusting to school, anger and aggression issues, and signs of depression.

In adolescence and adulthood, these consequences may be seen as alcohol and substance abuse, anxiety, signs of depression, social difficulties, strained familial relationships, running through multiple sexual partners, early sexual exploration, entering toxic and abusive romantic relationships, teen or young unplanned pregnancy, eating disorders, suicidal thoughts or attempts, distrust of others, and other symptoms of post-traumatic stress disorder.

Signs of post-traumatic stress disorder include:

1. *Re-experiencing traumatic events and symptoms— such as nightmares and flashbacks.*

2. *Memory loss.*

3. *Avoidance— purposefully or not, a person may avoid specific thoughts, emotions, people, or situations.*

4. *Insomnia and hypervigilance.*

5. *Specific fears.*

Signs You're Living in Survival Mode

Living in survival mode for so long can affect your daily life in what may seem like minor ways. The thing is, it can be hard even to know if you are living in survival mode. Below are some common signs that you have been experiencing "survival brain" for a prolonged period:

- Troubles focusing— When you try to read or get work done, things might seem foggy, or you might have a hard time focusing for long periods. You may have difficulties working on and concentrating on things you typically find easy. This may also be seen as zoning out in meetings or during conversations.

- Constant fatigue— Even after a good amount of sleep, recovery, or rest, you might still feel fatigued and exhausted.

- Experiencing impulsivity— After living in survival mode for so long, you may spend your money on random and frivolous items. For instance, eating more or taking risks that you normally wouldn't.

- Memory issues— You might have difficulty remembering names, faces, and things you need to do or losing items more quickly.

- Emotional reactivity— Experiencing extreme mood swings and heavier emotions about things that usually wouldn't upset you can signify that you are living in survival mode.

- Forgetting to care for your own needs— While you might find yourself caring for others, you may forget to exercise, brush your teeth, wash your clothes, or eat properly.

- Withdrawing and isolating yourself from the people around you— You may notice that you have stopped initiating meet-ups with friends and family, or that you no longer participate in activities you once loved.

- You're "jumpy"— The people around you may describe you as on edge, reactive, or jumpy.

- Having trouble trusting others— You may notice that you are suspicious of the people around you without having any good reason to be, and have trouble forming deep relationships.

All these signs of living in survival mode for too long can take a massive toll on your life and physical and mental health. If you see yourself in some of these descriptions, you now have a great starting point; all left is figuring out your survival mode "type" and how it manifests in your daily life. The section below will be a few exercises to get you started.

Ask the following questions to dig deeper into how you may be living in survival mode without even knowing it:

Which of the above signs do you relate with?

Would the people around you describe you as jumpy, excessively introverted, aggressive, or intensely people-pleasing? Whatever you relate most closely with might be your primary stress reaction.

What is Your Survival Mode?

How you learn to cope with stress and traumatic events develops in childhood, meaning that you are subconsciously living this way. You can rewire how you think, live, and react to situations around you. This will happen as soon as you realize that you are living in survival mode and what that means.

These survival modes and escape behaviors are also a way of avoiding facing or talking about hardships and trauma. As mentioned before, you couldn't help but develop them, and they were your one form of protection. But you no longer need to live like this.

The exercises below allow you to see what different survival modes look like. This part is about discovering what coping mechanisms you developed from childhood and preventing us from healing.

See the checklist below and note or mark down which of the following you experience or face:

1. Living in a state of denial

2. Rationalizing what has happened in the past, or making excuses as to why you are (or were) treated poorly.

3. Minimize things done or said to you (i.e., he or she said it was only a game)

4. Sowing disruption around you subconsciously

5. Self-harm

6. Being a perfectionist

7. Being abusive to others

8. Compulsive eating

9. Cutting yourself off from emotions and feeling numb

10. Exercising compulsively

11. Shoplifting

12. Avoid intimacy (physically or emotionally)

13. Have multiple personalities (masks)

14. Loss of memory and forgetting things regularly

15. The feeling that you leave your body (dissociation)

16. Feeling the need to always be in control

17. Gambling compulsively

18. Stayed busy without purpose or accomplishment

19. Abuse of alcohol/drugs

20. Being anorexic or bulimic

21. Hide behind your partner

22. Oversleeping

23. Having troubles sleeping

24. Relying on humor

25. Have rigid beliefs

26. Escaping or fleeing situations where you feel vulnerable (or even

safe)

27. Make suicide attempts

28. Avoid sexuality

29. Compulsive in sex

30. Being mentally absent (spacing out)

31. Always being alert of your surroundings, or being on guard (Hypervigilance)

32. Making excessive efforts to take care of others

33. Prostitution

Now that you have thought about and checked off different behaviors you find yourself struggling with, it's time to dive even deeper. These are all coping mechanisms used to protect you in the past. They are what your brain reverts to.

This means that when you notice these behaviors, you can tell when you exist in constant survival mode. Understanding why you experience these behaviors is a great step toward healing. Feel free to ponder and answer the questions below to continue this exercise:

How do you feel when you see the behaviors (and survival modes) checked off?

_____

_____

_____

Which survival mode has harmed you (mentally or physically), and how?
Was this in the past or present (or both)?

_____

_____

_____

Is there one mode or behavior that you are fine with experiencing? If so,
why?

_____

_____

_____

Now that you know some of your avoidance behaviors may be related to
your trauma and sexual abuse, how do you feel? Is there any part of you
that is relieved to see the reason behind it?

_____

_____

_____

18

FEELINGS AND SURVIVAL MODE

Setting goals for your healing is essential to tracking your progress, having something to work for, and focusing your energy on the right actions. Your goals will be personal and need to feel relevant to what you want to accomplish.

It's time for you to take over the recovery process fully. You have so much knowledge about healing, so now you just need to put that knowledge to use. Goals will help you move to new levels of recovery and keep you on track with the healing process.

What are Goals, and Why Are Goals Important?

Goals work to give you a sense of direction in your journey. Without them, you may end up spinning your wheels and never gaining traction. Even having small goals to get you started is better than having none at all.

To set goals for yourself is to create a roadmap to your future. When you can see clearly where you are going, you will develop motivation, fuel, and excitement about moving forward - having milestones to look forward to works to help the state of your trauma.

Even the smallest of goals give you a sense of accomplishment. When you slowly integrate little steps, your big recovery goals will be on the way faster than you could have ever imagined!

Goals are not wishes. They are simple, tangible actions you put your time and energy into making happen. They don't need to be extravagant, and they don't need to amaze the people around them. They inspire you to keep going, help you focus your mind, and give you hope and confidence.

It is important to note that when you begin setting goals, the journey is just as important as hitting your milestones. Enjoy the path you have created, focus your mind each day on what you are accomplishing, and watch as your goals become your reality!

How to Set Healing Goals

When you have the tools to begin healing, all that's left is being intentional with the process and creating the right goals. To set specific goals for healing, there are some things you need to keep in mind:

1. Make them achievable and realistic.

It can be easy to let our imaginations get the best of us. While allowing yourself to dream is good, you must learn to keep your goals realistic. It is admirable to have big goals, but if they are too vague or hard to reach, you may not find the motivation to do so. This means that when setting goals, make them something you can easily measure. When you have a specific goal, a set of steps to follow, and you can reach it within a set period, you have an attainable goal! It will feel a lot less overwhelming to start and keep you motivated to keep you going.

2. Personalized

Your goals need to feel close to your heart because if you don't relate to the result, you will not have the inspiration to reach them. When you begin setting healing goals, don't set them for other people or based on others. You need to be sure you are listening to your specific needs and recovery desires you you can create successful goals.

3. Collaborate with the people around you.

Yes, your goals need to be personal. However, allowing the people around you to help support you in your journey is just as essential. Your goals will be even more effective if you work with a therapist, close family, or friend who can help you reach your aspirations. They can help you refine and develop your goals and keep you accountable through collaboration.

4. Make them flexible

Goals should be checked regularly and re-negotiated when needed. When you can follow your goals and allow space for flexibility, you can shift your actions based on your needs. Your goals are not set in stone forever, and letting them evolve as you do is the best way to ensure they suit you best.

My first goal was to be able to give a name to my emotions. I wanted to continue doing the grounding practice above throughout the day as often as needed. Then, recognizing my responsibility in discussions with my partner started to come more easily (not always, but it was a step forward). I began understanding the importance of not waiting to explode when expressing myself. Work still needs to be done every day, and there is still a long way to go, but it's much better than before. We even managed to discuss wills and what we would do after each other's death. However, not too much. He has a Cartesian mind. I have a problematic relationship with money, which is anxiety-provoking. I try to enter those conversations in small doses.

When trying to discover the goals you want to set, I recommend the below questions and prompts as a great starting place:

What is bothering me in my current life that has led me to want to heal the wounds of sexual abuse? (make a list)

What are the current problems?

What have I learned about myself since I started reading this book?

What surprised me the most?

What will be different when the effects of sexual abuse are less present in your life?

What do you plan to do once the problems of sexual abuse are less present?

What would be your healing goal? (list a behavior or concrete action)

What indicator would tell that your goal is achieved?

Name one of your best qualities.

19

TO TELL ABOUT

The corrupt vision of actions will stay in our psyche for a long time. We were lied to; we were violated and hurt. This was not some fun game, nor was it fair. It was horrifying and disgusting. Then, the threats come, and we will be to blame if we talk about them. This is all our fault, or that is what we were told. All of it ended up destroying whatever confidence we had left in ourselves.

We are not responsible for other people's emotions, only ours. They do not belong to us. When they don't believe us, that is their own choice. It does not change what happened, and it does not change the fact that we need help.

As children, we felt responsible for the pain of the people around us when we talked about these things. The reactions of the people around us had us blaming ourselves, living in deep shame for decades.

The Importance of Talking About It

How family, friends, and parents react to someone speaking up about their abuse is decisive in the victim's healing process. This is why there is so much fear in opening up. Not being believed or their pain is minimized will destroy an adult or child's faith in all the people they love and trust.

This halts the healing process and could take them back to square one. Even if these negative repercussions are possible, speaking up about your experience is essential to healing. You must remember that childhood sexual abuse is a criminal act that should not be minimized or overlooked. Your hurt is valid, and you need to be able to express your pain in healthy ways to move forward in healing.

Exposing the facts, your emotions, and your experience is a massive part of the healing process. It is important to do this with someone you are sure will listen to you, believe your story, and support you in your desire to speak out.

It is best to do this as soon as possible. But this healing step can still take years or decades after the abusive acts have occurred. It is never too late to free ourselves from the guilt that is not ours. It is never too late to speak up.

Silence will only work to breed guilt and fear. Furthermore, it will block you from recovering. Dr. Mark Stevens, director of the University Counseling Services, said that the number one variable in how sexual assault can impact a person's life is whether the person keeps silent about it (Oh, 2012).

By keeping yourself quiet, no matter when it happens, you are giving your abuser triumph over you. They will grow confident that they have gotten away with their actions over time. Simply talking about what happened to a trusted family member or friend can make others aware of this person and how dangerous they are. Your openness about your trauma and experience will be beneficial, not only to you but, to the people around your abuser.

How Can You Speak Up?

Even if you crave opening up about your experience, you might not know where to start. I would first like to say that every experience, family situation, and the victim is different. Your story will not be the same as mine or another survivor, but that shouldn't stop you from stepping forward and sharing your story. Here are some steps you can take to feel more comfortable and confident when you decide to speak up:

Choose someone who you can fully trust— If you have never shared your story with anyone before or if you have and were not believed, you need to make sure you are confiding in someone you can trust.

When you are confident that you can trust this person to listen to you and not tell your story for you, they are the right person. This could be a mental health professional or a close family member. Whoever it is, you need to be comfortable with them and completely trust their word. This alone will make sitting down and speaking up so much easier.

When you should share— The person you decide to talk to needs to be showing you their full attention, they need to be in the right headspace, and they need to be available to talk for a while. It would be better to sit down with your confidante when they don't have anything to do after, are not distracted, and are not exhausted after a long day. You need to allow them to give you their undivided attention.

Where do you sit down together— The place you talk about your experience is also important to sharing and healing. This needs to be a space where you are comfortable and not naturally stressed. The space you choose should also be private to keep these conversations private. Randomly, a public area isn't the best spot to start sharing about this.

How you want to go about it is all up to you. If you want to do it in person, over the phone, or on a trip is your choice. Just be sure to note where, when, and with whom you feel most comfortable.

Moving forward in this process, you can brainstorm different spaces, people, and methods. But you also must consider your experiences and fears surrounding sharing your story.

Below are some questions to dive deeper into and reflect upon how you can move forward:

Have you ever spoken to anyone about the sexual abuse you suffered?

_____

_____

_____

Were you believed?

_____

What happened after?

What would be the next thing for you to do right now?

Do you feel the need to get away from certain members of your family, your friends, or your surroundings?

Is it easier to open up to someone you don't know?

Who in your life do you trust the most?

What feelings emerge when you imagine yourself finally opening up if you have never shared your story?

_____

_____

_____

Talking to a Professional

If you don't feel like you can trust anyone around you or simply don't want to talk to a family member or friend about your trauma, a therapist, or counselor may be a good choice for you. The important thing is claiming your truth, speaking up, and expressing your feelings to someone.

Childhood sexual abuse causes a lot of emotional turmoil and distress that needs to be released in some way. Therapists and counselors have the professional tools you need to be able to express your feelings and experiences while discovering more tools for how you can heal. There are many benefits to therapy as a way of speaking up. Here are some ways you can benefit from this healing tool:

Regaining control of your coping mechanisms— Unfortunately, it is very common for people who have experienced childhood sexual abuse to turn to dangerous coping mechanisms. This may include drug or alcohol abuse, self-isolation, or other methods of numbing oneself. Through therapy, you can learn healthy ways to process your feelings, speak about your struggles in a safe environment, and hear that your hardships are valid.

Reclaiming your sexual power— When you speak about your trauma to a therapist, you can learn how to take back the power of your sexuality! Talking about your needs, fears, and struggles means your therapist can guide you toward rediscovering your sexual power and beauty.

Learning how to move past your trauma— While talking to a family member is great, they don't have the proper qualifications or resources to guide you. They will listen to you without judgment and offer input when you want or need it. PTSD is very common in survivors of childhood sexual abuse, and therapists are equipped to help victims through it.

Taking back the power— These benefits work together to give you back your power. There is power in telling your story, even if it is just to one person. Many feel powerless after experiencing abuse, and these feelings can destroy their mental health. Therapy can help you say your experiences aloud and give you the right tools to regain strength.

20

WRITE AND BREAK FREE

"Society has made sexual assault the only crime where the perpetrator feels innocent and the victim guilty." —Benoîte Groulx, French journalist, novelist, and feminist activist.

What is Writing Therapy?

There are different ways of practicing writing therapy to work through trauma. It can be done online, in person, without a template, or guided (like the exercise we will do later).

If you feel like your abuser has all the power, but you can't speak up, this may be a great option. It is time that you reclaim your power, and it is time for you to take back control of your life.

Therapeutic writing, or writing therapy, is a form of expressive writing. This is a form of therapy where people are encouraged to talk about their experiences, thoughts, feelings, and emotions— especially regarding trauma and adverse childhood experiences (The Human Condition, 2023). It can be used for many people with many needs. We just talked about how speaking up is healing, which is another fantastic form of doing so.

You might be thinking that this just sounds like typical journaling, but it goes deeper than that. It seems like a simple practice, but writing in a diary or journal is typically free-form, where you write down your day and random things that pop into your head. On the other hand, writing therapy is a way of intentionally processing emotions, expressing yourself, and healing.

Have you ever tried typical journaling? If so, how did it go? If not, what has stopped you in the past?

Do you feel comfortable talking to someone about your trauma? If not, how do you feel about this writing option?

Different Forms of Writing Therapy

As I have mentioned, there are many ways you can practice writing as a form of therapy. To start, there are two main categories of writing therapy— guided by a licensed mental healthcare professional and self-motivated (The Human Condition, 2023). We will be covering the self-motivated version in this book. However, contact a professional if you are interested in the earlier option.

Below are some ways to practice therapeutic writing:

- Meditation and reflection on a specific experience, then journaling about what you felt.

- Songwriting.

- Free writing about a particular emotion, thought, or experience. This includes writing anything and everything that comes to mind as you reflect.

- Letter writing to your abuser, yourself, or a friend or family member to express the things you can't yet say.

- Writing out a list of the things you wish you could say but don't

Benefits of Writing Therapy

If you have trouble verbalizing your emotions and experiences, writing is a great practice for expressing yourself and speaking your truth. For people who have experienced traumatic events, this is a way for them to organize their thoughts and understand their emotions.

Writing about your trauma, thoughts, and feelings can help people to find meaning and purpose in hard times, develop new perspectives, and brainstorm ways to continue the healing process.

This kind of therapy has been connected to the improvement of the following conditions and mental illnesses, as well as other benefits (Ackerman, 2022):

- Soothing stress and anxiety

- Decrease symptoms of depression

- Eating disorder recovery

- Substance abuse

- Low self-esteem

- Post-traumatic stress disorder

- Communication skill issues

- Struggles with grief and loss

- Easing resentments and developing forgiveness

- Decreasing sleep struggles

- Finding answers and clarity

- Reduced levels of emotional (as well as physical) distress

- Healing emotional wounds you might not have known about

- Gaining closure and moving forward

A writing exercise:

Now is the time for you to blame the real culprit, through a writing exercise, in the form of a letter. Such an exercise can be very liberating. It consists of putting on paper everything you have felt from experience until now. Write down all the emotions (fears, pain, anger, betrayal, disappointment, etc.). Name what this violence has caused in your life.

Talk about the difficulties you face daily. Write down what you lost because of their actions (innocence, trust, sense of security).

You will address the person (or persons) who committed these criminal acts against you, using "I" statements as much as possible. It might sound like, "I was a kid, and you hurt me." You are going to write down how you felt at the time of the sexual abuse.

If you feel like you can't write a letter to your abuser just yet, you can also direct your thoughts to people who haven't protected or believed you. Just do it at your own pace, taking breaks whenever needed, without giving up.

No matter how difficult, writing this letter will bring a new sense of healing and closure. It is an act of facing your fears, and you will prove that you can do it! So even though this letter only contains a few sentences, it is progress, and you can always add more. And why not tell him what you have decided to do with your relationship with them? Tell them you're going to cut ties and heal on your own or whatever else you decide. It's a way to regain control of your life.

How:

Set aside a time when you won't be distracted or interrupted. Then sit down in a quiet space with a pen and paper. Prepare your mind to enter where you have experienced trauma and stress. Take a deep breath and get going.

You can now decide to burn it, tear it into a thousand pieces, or destroy it in another way. This writing exercise can be done whenever the need arises.

Let's dive into some questions and reflect on what you experienced through this process.

How does it feel after this exercise?

Do you need to move or relax?

_____

_____

Do you feel like you need to repeat the process while addressing someone else?

_____

_____

What feelings did this exercise arise in you?

_____

_____

Other Writing Prompts

It is important that you practice multiple techniques when discovering therapeutic writing. When you find yourself stuck or not wanting to re-do the exercise above, here are some other ways you can practice writing to heal:

- Write a poem about a specific emotion and how it feels (both physically and emotionally)

- Write a letter to your younger self

- Write a letter to your future self, asking how healing feels. Then write a reply, stepping into the shoes of your future self, as if you have reached a better place already.

- Write about how you felt as a child regarding your trauma vs. how you feel now

- What areas of your life have been affected by this abuse?

- Write about how your trauma affects you daily.

- Write an entry as if you were first talking to someone about your abuse. What would you say? How freeing would it feel?

- Who is one person in your life you know you can trust to speak the truth to you? What would they say to you if you talked to them about your childhood sexual abuse experience?

- Connect with your inner child and write a note that (if you could) you would leave on their pillow after the abuse happened.

- Describe yourself in ten words, none of which connect you to your abuse. How do these words make you feel?

If you can't bring yourself to follow a prompt, then allow yourself to free-write and follow wherever your mind leads. Let your brain run wild, express everything you feel at this moment, what you have felt in the past, and dream about the future. Whatever you write is what your mind needs to get out!

21

DEVICTIMIZATION

Even after shifting the guilt for the criminal acts onto the abusers, the scars left behind can last years, even a lifetime. Your scars are proof that you survived, and they are proof that you have started healing. But these scars are not supporting you in your continued healing.

They are seen in many ways, one of which is the inability to take charge of oneself and to flourish independently. Many victims are unable to get and preserve long-term employment. I include myself in the lot. This is not for lack of trying.

Being financially dependent keeps us in a mindset of asking for our needs to be met. Conflicts are, therefore, likely to be more frequent, with the provider assuming all financial responsibilities. There is no doubt that this kind of link is doomed to rout in the more or less short term.

Now, here are the disadvantages of being taken care of.

- We live in fear

- We see everything negatively

- We remain guilt

- We have a feeling of incompetence

- We have a feeling of shame

- We have low self-esteem

- We are isolated

- We lack self-confidence

- We develop a passivity

- Diseases develop

I didn't want to live as I did before. I wanted to get out of the "victim mode," and it was time to regain my independence. In the group sessions, we were obviously told that the responsibility for sexual acts was not our fault.

However, it is our responsibility to heal and become survivors rather than victims. This stage of healing is called de-victimization. The wound left by these traumatic experiences can be healed because it is no longer completely crippling.

Through the process of healing wounds, you can:

- Have less guilt

- Finally have a sense of freedom

- Take back control of your life

- Choose the people around us

- Decide your situations

- Fully understand your needs

- Dare to ask for things

- Be positive

- Be independent

- Be safe and feel safe

- Become aware of our strengths and weaknesses

- Take concrete actions

- Have higher levels of self-confidence

- Take care of our mental and physical health

- Release your energy how you want

- Learn to love yourself

Which of these benefits would you like to receive first (top 3)? And Why?

Do you feel like you are living your life independently? If so, in what areas? If not, how do you want to start?

You're A Survivor

The healing journey transforms you from victim to survivor. Mindset is the most significant difference between these two identities. Although you had no choice to go through these traumatic events and be a victim, you have the power to grow and become a thriving survivor.

When you can't get into the "I survived, and I'm more powerful than I ever thought" mindset, you won't be able to break free from the victimhood stage. The survivor mentality is about acknowledging that you have survived trauma and that every small victory of healing, affirmation, or respect inspires you to continue healing. It doesn't always mean having a positive attitude, but it does mean continuing to find your way.

Another word I like to use for survivors is a warrior. You have struggled to get to this point in your recovery and deserve to be proud of yourself. Warriors fight and survive, even if they are victims of violence. Going from a victim to a survivor to a warrior will not be an easy path. But it will be so liberating on your healing journey!

Getting Out of "Victim Mode"

When you are stuck in the mindset that there is nothing you can do because there was nothing you could do in the past, healing will be much harder. Getting out of "victim mode" means taking back your power, knowing that there are things you are in control of and that you get to write your story now. Let's dive deeper into a few tangible ways to break free from this cycle and escape living in "victim mode."

Recognize the cycle of self-sabotage - Self-sabotage is both highly destructive and extremely addicting.

- Do you stop yourself from doing things you love or need to do because of anxiety?

- Do you neglect your mental and physical health?

- Are you consistently procrastinating?

If you answered *yes* to any of these things, you are likely self-sabotaging daily. Living in constant victim mode and self-sabotage means a few things:

- Limited potential as a professional (Green Hypose, 2021)

- Exhausting your spouse and friends with complaints

- Limiting the potential of your leisure activities

- Holding yourself back from healing

It is easy to pity oneself, to believe that there is nothing more we can do. But all this does is sabotage our pursuits in healing before they have even started. Simply realizing that you are stuck in this cycle is a massive step forward because it means you are no longer in denial (Green Hypose 2021).

Practice small forms of independence in the beginning— Complete independence will not come overnight. Like everything in the healing process, you need to be patient and take it one step at a time. Here are some ways to learn and practice small acts of independence:

- Pick up a hobby, or engage in an activity you enjoy— by yourself. This could be painting, writing, a dance class, cooking class, pilates, taking a bath, going to the beach, getting a coffee alone, or many other things. No matter what you like to do, try to do it alone once or twice a week. It will become easier over time, and making bigger leaps will be much less daunting.

- Learn practical communication skills— Discovering how to articulate your thoughts and needs is essential to de-victimize yourself, regain your power, and becoming more independent. Practicing expressing your thoughts will help you become aware of your needs, set clear boundaries, and let others know that you will not be walked all over anymore. Practicing saying no is a great way to start this step. When you can protect your time and do what you want, your communication skills will shine through!

- Try spending intentional time with yourself. Being alone, reading a book, meditating, exercising, or walking, and existing with your thoughts will make you more comfortable with yourself. When you are confident with just being alone, independence will naturally follow. And when you can confidently listen to yourself, breaking free from victimization will be on the way.

- Take Back Power—One of the best ways to stop living as a victim is to take back responsibility for your life. You cannot change what happened in the past, and you have no power to prevent the trauma you have been through. But you now have the power to take responsibility for your future. You will always experience difficulties and struggles, and healing will not be easy.

However, when you see yourself living and acting independently and powerfully, your confidence will grow! It's time to take a proactive stance in the movie that is your life, making decisions to heal rather than instinctively reacting to what's thrown at you.

You can start doing this by celebrating your small and big wins! When you acknowledge the progress you are making in some area of your life, you will be able to gain confidence in yourself and your strength. A great way to do this is to keep a journal to record your daily, weekly, and monthly earnings. Celebrate spending time alone, having a difficult conversation, or even cooking a meal for yourself!

Relying on temporary outside help - While independence is important in breaking free from victimhood, admitting that you need a little help is just as essential. You won't be able to do it all alone, and recognizing that is an excellent show of strength. There are no rules for asking for small amounts of help. You might find comfort in a friend, family member, therapist, or group therapy session.

Changing your mindset from victim to warrior is difficult, but it will be necessary. You've survived everything that's happened to you. With the tools above, you can relearn how to live independently and celebrate your progress!

There may be days when you still feel like a victim, and there will be days when you feel like you barely survived. But these are only calls for rest, the rest of the warrior. Each day brings its share of difficulties, but you are better and better equipped. Therefore, you are stronger than ever.

22

FEEL EMOTIONS

"While the emotion gives energy which is translated into a bodily movement and lasts only a few minutes, the feelings color the thoughts in a more lasting way." —*Isabelle Filliozat*, author and psychotherapist.

I like this definition of emotions. It illustrates the reaction produced by emotion greatly. Emotions drive many people to do things their conscious brain may not do, and they transform the way we see the world and perceive ourselves.

In fact, emotions don't only affect our thoughts. They are contagious. Frequently, when the people around us are happy, that influences us. On the other hand, when the people we grow up with are angry, aggressive, or on edge, that can also transfer over to us.

The phrase "misery loves company" is so accurate. When one person, parent, friend, or spouse is miserable, they may subconsciously drag you down with them. This is important to remember when stepping into the phase of processing emotions. You need to differentiate if they are your feelings or if they were given to you.

Despite where they come from, they are valid, and you still need to process them. But knowing how you developed and started feeling certain emotions (often through survival modes) can help you understand yourself better and move toward healing.

The next step in healing in this workbook will be about your emotions. We have discussed the emotions connected to survival modes, but understanding and experiencing your feelings is just as important.

Since childhood, we have pushed aside our emotions because feeling them meant reliving the trauma, which hurts. It was a coping mechanism, but we don't need that anymore.

You are safe now, so it's time to understand better the different emotions and how you can talk about them. Because when you can sit with your emotions, understand them, and express them, you will begin healing your emotional side and inner child.

The Five Primary Emotions and How to Talk About Them

The five primary human emotions are happiness, sadness, fear, disgust, and anger. You might think, "I feel much more than just those five!" But it is crucial to remember that these are just the core, and other emotions flow from these.

Excitement comes from happiness, regret comes from sadness, and embarrassment comes from fear. Scientists are still debating over how many categories of emotions there are, but these five pillars are a great framework to start with.

We will go over the five primary emotions together. Then we will explore how you can talk about and process them, then have an exercise to brainstorm other emotions you are experiencing through that specific primary emotion.

Understanding your emotions and how normal and human they are will be revolutionary for your healing journey. In this section, you will be equipped with the tools to dive deeper into understanding your feelings and.

Happiness

Happiness is an emotion that people generally enjoy the feeling of. We like to feel calm, joyful, and in a positive mood. You will find yourself mimicking or expressing happiness through laughing, smiling, doing something you enjoy, or indulging yourself.

Below are some situations when happiness is cultivated:

- When you are surrounded by people who genuinely love, validate, and appreciate you.

- Experiencing feelings of security, comfort, and safety.

- When you are experiencing an activity that absorbs all of your attention and brings you joy.

- Deeply experiencing feelings of peace and relaxation.

- When you participate in an activity that triggers sensory pleasure, such as eating a nice meal, exercising, or doing something you love.

Pop culture likes to make us think that buying a house, a new car, or a designer bag will make us happy, but that is not the reality. This emotion is highly individualized and is not necessarily based on outside influences (just as material items). It is linked to mental and physical health, so genuine happiness will follow when you take the time to improve these aspects of your life.

Learning to express and talk about feelings needs to start simply and easily. It might seem obvious that you say joy when experiencing happiness, but understanding the terminology and words you can use is the foundation of proper emotional understanding and expression.

That being said, you can use the following terms to describe joy and happiness when you talk about it: love, relief, peace, satisfaction, pride, joy, excitement, amusement, humor, and contentment.

Now it's time to do some brainstorming for yourself. Answer the questions below to dig deeper into happiness and your understanding:

When do you feel true happiness, contentment, joy, and peace? Now take some time to describe a few of your happiest moments:

Is there something in you that believes you can't feel happiness? If so, what do you think is blocking you? (i.e., feelings of stress, worry, anxiousness, etc.)

When was the last time you can remember feeling truly happy?

What sub-categories of happiness do you experience the most? (i.e., humor, peace, relaxation, excitement, etc.)

Sadness

This is another emotion that we all feel from time to time. However, the severity of this sadness is what varies. A specific event or memory, such as a loss, rejection, or another negative or traumatic event, may cause this emotion.

On the other hand, there may be times when you have no idea why you're feeling sad, just that you are. Sometimes, when people experience prolonged periods of sadness, this emotion can turn into depression.

No one expresses sadness the same every time they experience this emotion. You might find yourself crying, becoming quiet, withdrawing from social events, having a dampened mood, feeling fatigued or lethargic, or having difficulty sleeping. The type, severity, and expression of sadness all depend on the root cause of the feeling.

To adequately express and communicate your sadness, here is some terminology you can become familiar with: gloomy, lonely, depressed, resigned, miserable, unhappy, lost, hopeless, disappointed, heartbroken, and grieving.

Sadness can be challenging to work through when you have experienced childhood trauma, but understanding the root cause is the first step in moving forward. Feel free to fill in and answer the question below to learn more about yourself and your sadness. These can be good questions to ask repeatedly and regularly:

Right now, describe everything you are thinking about regarding your sadness:

Did something specific trigger this sadness to arise? If so, are you sad about that trigger, or is it something deeper?

How have you been feeling, generally, this past week? Has this sadness been persistent?

Have you allowed yourself to mourn what you may be missing or sad about?

What is one *small,* positive, feel-good activity you could do today to help yourself cope and feel even just one percent better?

.

Fear

The feeling of fear occurs when your mind or body senses any sort of threat. Fear lies in our instincts and, fundamentally, helps us survive. Again, this feeling varies in severity depending on the perceived threat.

However, it is essential to note that sometimes the level of the fear does not equally match the intensity of the danger before you. People who have experienced childhood abuse often develop high levels of anxiety and an increased sense of fear. Anxiety means you experience fear in situations that may not pose much threat. Even though the fear may not match the threat, that doesn't make the feeling any less real.

Just like with every other emotion, people experience fear differently. That is why many different survival modes exist, including four primary stress responses. Fear will do something different to each individual. Some people might be more sensitive to specific triggers, while others seek out thrills and fear for enjoyment.

Objects, situations, people, and conversations, among other things, can all trigger fear. Just know that if you experience fear and your logical brain tells you it is unimportant, you still feel a valid emotion. No matter what happens, your brain may be in or entering fight or flight mode, which is very high-stress and vulnerable.

Fear can manifest as phobias, panic attacks, general self-isolation, social or general anxiety, hypervigilance, and the inability to perceive the world around you logically. Fear keeps you locked in survival mode, and it's time to learn how to break free.

To be able to talk about your fear and triggers, you need to be equipped with different terminology regarding fear. The following words describe other forms of this feeling: stressed, desperate, anxious, doubtful, terrified, panicked, confused, horrified, worried, nervous, and scared.

To continue to cope with fear and move forward toward healing, here are some small steps you can take regularly:

- Confront little fears rather than avoiding them— This does not need to start with your greatest fears. If you are afraid of serious discussions, public speaking, driving, meeting new people, or roller coasters, take time regularly to face these fears. When you do this enough, your brain will understand that you are stronger than your fears and that they do not control your life.

To practice this step, I did a few small things. My spouse and I would talk about money, which is a susceptible subject for me and a source of anxiety. I knew we had to have these kinds of discussions.

However, many times I fled when it came to talking about money. But when I decided to start facing my fears, I remained seated. I took deep breaths and listened. When I could speak on a point, I agreed to continue calmly. It's difficult for me to this day. But I am aware of my difficulty. I ask for time before exchanging; then, I choose the moment.

- If you can face it, distract yourself. Sometimes fears are too much to face, so distraction is your only option to get through an intense moment of fear or anxiety. Rather than letting your thoughts and fear meditate, a good way to distract yourself can be through listening to an audiobook, going on a walk, playing music, watching a movie, going to the gym, practicing art, or even cooking a new recipe.

- Try to consider your fear from a logical standpoint— If it is possible at the moment, try to take a step back and think about your fear. Is this something that can emotionally or physically harm you? What worst-case scenario could happen if this threat could hurt you? When you think about this, ponder what you would do in that situation. When you can know what actions you will take, it can help you get past specific fears. This can be a tough step at the beginning of your healing journey. Sometimes it will take a while to learn how to manage your fear rationally, which is okay. This is not an impossible feat, but allow time for this one.

Let's journal and ask some questions each time you feel the emotion of fear or anxiety to understand yourself better:

Is this fear something that happened in your past? If so, how likely is it to happen to you again?

Did something (a person, word, experience, or object) trigger your anxiety or feelings of fear?

Have you ever been harmed (physically or emotionally) by this threat you are anxious about? If so, what can you do to help protect yourself from being hurt again?

Disgust

Disgust is a natural human reaction and feeling that comes from experiencing something unwanted or unpleasant. While this might sound like an odd emotion to have as a primary emotion, the feeling of disgust protects us and keeps us from danger. Our bodies are repulsed by the smell of rotting food, which keeps us from eating it and getting sick.

However, the feeling of disgust can be inaccurate and manipulative if you have low self-esteem or a warped view of the world around you. Without knowing why you might not like someone else or yourself, and this is when this emotion can become a problem.

Regarding terminology, disgust can also be described as aversion, withdrawal, nauseating, uncomfortable, hate, dislike, disturbing, offense, disapproval, and loathing.

While disgust can be very helpful, there are going to be times when you want to overcome it, so here are some things you can do:

Practice slow exposure— Some things you will never grow to like, and that's okay. However, if you struggle to enjoy something from childhood due to trauma but desire to find joy in them, this exercise is for you!

You don't have to go all out and do things that will make you spiral, but listening to what your inner child wants is a significant step. Slowly, without forcing, listen to if your disgust leads you to react strongly. If you begin to feel overwhelmed, withdraw. You are under no obligation to continue.

Practice deeper compassion— Sometimes, if you look in the mirror and want to change something. Even further, it is easy to dislike someone for no reason. But in these situations, compassion is the practice that must be implemented.

When you use affirming words in the mirror, you can learn to trust and love yourself more. And when you try to put yourself in someone else's shoes, you can also discover compassion for them.

Below are questions you can ask yourself when you are feeling the emotion of disgust:

Is there something in your past that you are relating to this present experience? If so, why do you believe disgust is triggered at this moment in time?

.

When you experience disgust (on a small or large level), what words typically come to mind?

.

Do these specific words have any link to your past traumas?

When you know the source of initial disgust in your past... what steps will you take to improve your reaction and feelings toward certain situations?

Anger

Anger is the final primary emotion we will discuss in this chapter. This feeling most often occurs when we experience an injustice of any sort. When this happens, you may also experience feelings of defenselessness, feeling threatened or trapped, and a fear of being unable to defend yourself.

Many believe that anger is only a negative emotion; if it sits too long and unaddressed, it can be. But anger, when channeled in new ways, can become a source of power and an agent of change. Anger can help you know when a situation or relationship is abusive or toxic. It can aid your escape and give you the gut feelings and power to leave.

Feelings of anger can also look like an annoyance, frustration, irritation, mad, vengeance, cheating, insult, bitterness, and infatuation.

Dealing with anger is not a "one size fits all" thing, and you may need to experiment with different strategies until you find something that works well for you. Next up, we'll go over some ways you can learn to manage and cope with feelings of anger and frustration.

Take a break— Taking a break doesn't just mean closing your eyes and taking a deep breath. It means gaining distance between you and the situation angering you. When things get too heated, your emotions may lead you towards a destructive path rather than a constructive one. If you want to use your anger to change what is happening, you need to reconsider yourself, take a break, and avoid in-the-moment reactions. Responses are well-thought-out and helpful in situations and conversations where things might get intense. So just remember response vs. reaction. If the problem you are in is triggering you and causing you to re-experience your trauma, taking a break is the best thing you can do for yourself. Let those emotions cool down, then allow yourself to re-enter calmly.

Use constructive language to communicate anger— Many people who experienced childhood trauma will hold in their rage to prevent further conflicts. Internalizing this anger might feel like you are keeping other people from getting hurt.

Still, the reality is that you are just hurting yourself even more. This works to keep your anger bubbling and may lead to broken relationships and grudges. So, rather than taking time to cool off, then brushing it aside, try to come back to the conversation calmly.

Let them know that they hurt you, that you disagree, or that you think they should have done something differently. Always leave a line of communication open and let them know you want to hear their side. This can help you use your anger in constructive and healthy ways.

Focus your energy on finding a solution— The feeling of anger can give you a lot of energy and adrenaline. So, rather than using this energy in ways you may have in the past, try to channel it to find a solution. This can be a lot easier said than done. Working to find a solution can look like expressive writing to get all the pent-up emotions out and work towards finding a way out. Feelings of anger can bring up past trauma and make you feel like a helpless child again. But that doesn't mean you need to feel like this forever. Take back that power and use it to work with people or yourself to find solutions to existing and previous issues.

A Grounding Technique

(This exercise allowed me to get out of "victim mode")

When learning about your emotions and how they affect you, discovering ways to ground yourself amid the storm is one of the most important things I have learned through my healing journey.

Even four years after discovering this grounding technique, I have maintained good relationships with my boyfriend, co-workers, and customers. I don't react emotionally to negative comments anymore. It has saved my life— it transformed my life. I have been able to keep my job, I like my colleagues, and I can communicate with family without the old tension or fear. It's incredible how effective it has been. It's as though my past no longer colors my present with fear or sadness, which is so freeing.

Now, before I answer others with something negative because I feel ignored or rejected, I use this grounding technique. It may seem easy or too simple at first, but it helped me gain trust in my emotions and make more conscious decisions.

Making peace with your emotions and learning to sit with them is a massive goal of healing. But if you cannot feel your emotions and ground yourself when you experience them, how will you ever make peace with them? If you can never make peace with your emotions, they will wreak havoc on your life. They will continue to control your actions and halt your recovery.

Discovering how to make peace with what you feel is not the only reason grounding techniques are useful. Re-centering yourself can help you be more mindful and aware of the world and life around you, giving you the tools to improve yourself.

If your feet are not planted firmly beneath you, it can be hard to concentrate on the important things, keep yourself on the healing journey, and recognize how your emotions drive your actions daily.

Our world is troubled, and your past has caused you to lose balance, and grounding techniques are a way of restoring that peace and balance. Through more practice, you will be able to become more self-aware and comfortable finding solutions to problems through self-reflection.

It is important to note that so many different grounding techniques exist. The one I am sharing with you today is the one I have personally found the most success with. But feel free to expand with your practices and continue to discover other grounding methods. However, I would recommend choosing one to practice regularly. This is because it will become an automatic habit with enough time and practice.

Here's how you can practice this technique:

First, sit in a chair (or stand) with your feet planted flat on the ground. It helps me to imagine that my feet are rooted to the ground. This makes it so you can physically feel "grounded."

Second, look around you, taking a deep breath in and then out. From there, name five things you see around you. Then, name five things you hear. After this, name the emotion you feel at that moment. Not the emotion you felt earlier in the day, not the emotion you are anticipating, the emotion of this specific moment.

For example:

Five things I see: "I see a table, I see a chair, I see a plant, I see a door, I see a glass of water."

Five things I hear: "I hear the clock ticking, a car passing by, my breath, a child running outside, and the sound of the refrigerator." (If you can only hear less than five things, that's okay).

Then, calmly try to listen to your emotions. If you can't identify any emotion, do the technique again. This time, name four things you see and four things you hear. Now, try to name the emotion you feel at the moment. Repeat as many times as you need to feel more in touch with your surroundings and emotions.

It's possible that you won't be able to identify the emotion you are experiencing. This is normal among people with severe dissociative symptoms, just like me. It may take some time to feel or understand your emotion, but you will see your progress every time you try this technique. The first time might take you four sets of the technique. After a couple of weeks, you might only need two sets.

If you can, I recommend doing this exercise a few times daily. But if you can only manage one time a day, that's fine. It's about listening to your mind and body and connecting the two.

This practice has helped me during high-stress situations, even when I was on the go, in everyday life: in a waiting room, during the break at work, and even before clients reached my workspace. Luckily, practicing this technique daily will exercise your grounding muscle so that you can take a pause and recenter yourself naturally when you need to.

It took me three days of doing this exercise three times a day to name anger. Before this, I couldn't identify that I felt anger before I exploded with rage. Now, the more emotions I learn to identify, the easier it is for me to unlock my trauma, process it, and heal.

Be sure to remember that naming something reduces the power it has over you. Learning how to manage or control something reduces your fear of it. This grounding technique has helped me break free from discomfort and the urge to run away in the face of difficult emotions.

Even further, this is a great tool when you are overwhelmed by emotions and don't know how to act. Instead of reacting to your first impulse, you can stop and think about how you want to respond. With this benefit, you will gain greater control of yourself, your actions, and your life.

Contagious Emotions

Emotions don't appear out of the blue. They are most often triggered by external factors or passed onto us by the people around us. There are scientific reasons why you often feel the emotions of the people around you. It typically happens in three stages: mimicry, feedback, and experience (Raypole, 2019). The mimicry stage of taking on other people's emotions is connected to empathy and our mirror neurons.

Parts of us, deep inside, want to ease the pain or share in the joy of others. Children mimic emotions to experience them to learn what emotions and emotional regulation are. You are likely to have picked up on more negative emotions than positive ones. This is due to growing up in an abusive or strained family environment. How you experienced emotions as a child will still affect your life today, and that's why it is vital to take note of where your feelings stem from.

Below are the three phases of emotional contagion and how you can notice the pattern:

1. *Mimicry*

You must recognize a specific emotion to mimic it. However, since most emotional cues are subtle, this recognition of another person's emotions will often be subconscious. Children will quickly learn that yelling means anger and a smile means peace and happiness.

Mimicry often occurs through body language because those are the easiest cues to pick up on. Even further, people naturally gravitate toward mimicking the body language and nonverbal cues of people they admire.

When you are talking to a friend or partner, you might slowly start to notice that when they cross their arms, you do too. You might also find that when someone is getting angry, you furrow your brow. Mimicking helps humans relate to one another. It also means that you can develop deep connections to other people's emotions. This can be good or bad, depending on the emotions being transferred.

2. Feedback

Your mind and body are connected, so when your physical body starts to experience these emotional cues, your brain will offer feedback. Your crossed arms might soon make you tense, or the smile you plastered across your face might put you at ease.

You might notice that the feedback stage gets mixed up in children in abusive homes. This is where much guilt and confusion about childhood sexual abuse begins.

The people around you are happy and love the person who hurt you. Are those the emotions you are supposed to feel around them? Your mind and body connection through emotions can begin to get tangled up.

3. Contagion (or experience)

After your brain recognizes that your body is experiencing an emotion, your mind begins to feel and take it on as an emotion. This means that this anger and manipulation that was once your abuser is now internalized. This is when those external emotions are evoked in yourself and become "contagious."

This is the process of learning how to pick up on the emotions of others. Still, when you experience trauma in childhood, the process can get confusing. You may begin to relate hurtful emotions with happiness, leading to further confusion. Let's dive deeper into what emotions are and the primary ones you can look out for.

Childhood Emotional Needs

Emotional health is critical to our development as children and adults. When our emotional needs as children are not met, it will affect us for years and even decades after. With what we have gone through, our childhood needs were not met, which is why I include this section. This is here to pinpoint what you lacked as a child and what you can fight to cultivate now. Below are some of the basic emotional needs for children and how they affect us into adulthood (Newmark):

- Respect— Children need to be treated with kindness and courtesy. When they feel their needs, desires, and opinions are not respected, they will not learn to respect themselves or the people around them. Having experienced trauma in childhood, you were not respected, which will greatly affect how you view yourself and your needs.

- Importance and appreciation— As a child, you need to hear that you are useful and be treated like you are truly appreciated. When you don't receive this, you will likely experience low self-esteem as a child and an adult.

- Security— A child needs to feel safe, loved, protected, and cared for. If you don't receive this as a child, you will begin to live in survival mode. Everything is a threat, and there is no one to protect you but yourself.

- Acceptance— As a child, feel accepted and that your unique being is enough as you were created. Not experiencing this can cause a person to search for acceptance in other people or possibly substances that numb them later.

- Inclusion— Children need to be a part of something meaningful and bigger than themselves. This helps connect them to others, discover a sense of community, and cultivate social skills. When a home setting does not offer a sense of belonging, a child will seek it in other areas of their life, and it may often be found in unhealthy environments.

Not having been believed in childhood, the need for importance is the one to which I must pay particular attention. I often had the reflection while watching films: "why does this girl give herself so much importance?". The reality is that it was me who wasn't offering myself enough importance or value. I never knew how to go about meeting this need.

Five Steps to Sitting with Your Feelings

Every time you experience an emotion, you will notice it, but from that moment on is what matters. Learning how to sit with your emotions, processing them, and feeling them is necessary to healing, understanding yourself, and allowing yourself to see all the hurt you have experienced. Sitting with your feelings (not just seeing them and distracting yourself) is essential to learning how to cope with and process your trauma. Here are the five steps you can follow to discover how to sit with your feelings:

Recognize and admit you are feeling something. It might sound obvious, but this is a step we often forget about. You first need to learn how to admit that you are feeling something (negative or positive). We can get used to distracting ourselves and doing everything to avoid acknowledging that we are experiencing deep emotions.

Listen to what the emotion and your body have to say and give yourself the right to feel it— Your body will show you signs of what is happening in your subconscious mind. In this step, it is time to permit yourself to feel your emotions on a deeper level. It can be scary to dive deeper and feel more, but this is essential.

Give a name to your emotion— When you have given yourself the right to experience and feel your emotions, it's time to name them. Sometimes it can be hard to put a label on what feeling it is that we are experiencing, but that is where the five primary emotions listed above can come in handy! Just remember to start small. Is the feeling positive or negative? Or is it neutral? With more practice, you will be able to name your feelings as they pop up, it just takes some time.

Examine the situation and why you are reacting the way you are— Feelings are naturally internal experiences. But more often than not, they are triggered by an external situation. It can be hard, but stepping outside the internal processing of your emotions is necessary. You need to learn how to recognize what triggers certain emotions in you.

Why are you reacting the way you are? Is this reaction positive or negative?

Is your reaction causing you to feel other emotions?

_____

_____

Does it come from a trauma from your childhood?

_____

_____

Speak in "I" and not in "you." "I'm scared," "I'm hurt," and "I'm happy" are all examples of healthy "I" language that helps you process and express what you're going through. . The final step to sitting down with your emotions is to start speaking for yourself. Stop saying, "you caused this", whether to yourself or an external trigger. At this stage, you need to focus on your feelings and sensations.

What should I do when I feel numb?

In this next exercise, you will discover the times when numbness occurs. This is very important because it often happens without our knowledge. You know, when you realize you haven't been paying attention for a few minutes during a conversation? Your mind has drifted away. To what? You may not be sure. Or maybe in a stressful situation, you walk away not remembering what people around you even said.

It means that you have cut yourself off from your emotions. This is called dissociation. This coping mechanism helps us get through life without hurting ourselves more than we already have. It can cause arguments when you stop listening to the people around you or never seem to react to the emotional parts of stories.

Although you are not responsible for the emotions of others, not being attentive to yourself and them can lead to you isolating yourself from the people around you.

Staying focused can be difficult. But this is not the desired goal. Developing self-awareness and becoming more mindful is the beginning of learning to give yourself respect. It is also the beginning of respect for others.

You can start by explaining your difficulties and desire to solve a problem to those around you. People like to help. Expressing your needs can train your loved ones to be more sensitive and attentive to your needs. You are no longer a victim but a whole self-respecting person.

In the next exercise, you will work on identifying when you no longer pay attention to what is happening around you. This exercise will be helpful when you come out of a situation without remembering much of what happened.

Try writing these questions ahead of time on a piece of paper to keep with you. Have a pen with this sheet to answer when you need it. Ask yourself four simple questions:

- Where was I? _____
- With who? _____
- What's the last subject I remember? _____

  _____

- What was the emotion that caused the numbness?

  _____

You can redo this short questionnaire whenever this happens. You will see how it brings respect from others, and you will feel like part of the group.

Why Am I Losing Control?

Learning to recognize and name our emotions is a vital task for healing. However, feeling them is probably the most challenging part. Experiencing an emotion is not a bad thing in itself. Feeling angry is normal. It's a natural human emotion. It is not catastrophic to share it. It can be a great indicator that you need to pay attention to something bothering you. It is a tool that can be used to push us forward. We begin to treat it as a cry for help from our inner selves without judging or condemning it.

Actively learning to feel emotions may be new to some people. If you haven't been believed or supported in your past, anger at disapproval and disrespect from loved ones may still be internalized and show up from time to time.

Anger can make you feel like you are losing control of yourself. It can be scary to feel like everything is spiraling out of control. Still, feeling anger is the first step to regaining control. Give yourself the space to recognize it. You have good reason to be angry.

In the questions and prompts below, we'll explain how and why you feel overwhelmed and lost when angry.

List situations when you feel overwhelmed with anger.

How do you feel in your body when you feel angry?

What underlying feeling is causing your anger (guilt, abandonment, rejection, resentment)?

Do you have unmet needs?

  1. Physically (food, water, breathing, sleep, health)

  2. Security (security of body, job, resources, morals, family, property, health)

  3. Love or belonging (friendship, family, social interaction, intimacy, affection)

  4. Esteem (self-esteem, confidence, respect of and by others)

5. Self-actualization (passions, creativity, morality, problem-solving)

_____

_____

_____

_____

How do you usually react, when you feel angry? (i.e. crying, isolating yourself, physically injuring yourself, destroying your environment, etc.)

_____

_____

What is the result of your anger reactions?

_____

_____

_____

When you can finally recognize these things about your anger and the source of it, you will be able to work toward taking back your power. Just remember that you still deserve to feel angry about what has happened in your past. Next, we will discuss the signs your body might send you before you lose control.

What Signals Does my Body Send Before I Lose Control?

Our bodies let us know something is wrong when we cannot listen to what our brains tell us. When we can't trust the memories or stress responses our brains emit, it is time to turn to the physical signs.

Anger can make us lose control, anxiety can make us feel like we are spiraling, and sadness can make us feel like there is no way out of the darkness. But take solace in your body, letting you know that you are about to lose control.

You will experience physical signs of anger, such as shaking, increased heart rate, and muscle tightness. Then behavioral signs will also arise, such as impulsivity, physical aggression, and shouting will also arise.

Below are examples of my cues. This list has helped me to recognize what is happening before my brain fully alerts me.

My physical signs that announce my anger:

- Muscle contractions and tightness— specifically in my shoulders, hands, and gaze.

- Shortened, rapid breathing.

- Redness and heat flushing my cheeks, chest, and neck.

My behavioral cues of anger and losing control:

- Either speaking loud and harshly or going completely mute.

- Having a hard time making decisions, even small ones.

- Pouting and sulking.

Looking back at the list of feelings under the survival mode of alcohol abuse, this is exactly why I was drinking. I was unable to express my anger, and I felt rejected and made to feel guilty. I was passively cashing in.

Once fasted, I exploded. I didn't know any other way to express something was going wrong, and I didn't want to feel it anymore. Even more disconcerting, I couldn't name what triggered the anger.

Answer the questions and prompts below to dive deeper into discovering your signals:

Describe the last time you got angry:

How did your body feel? If you can't remember or pinpoint those details— how were you acting with the people around you?

Do you often react a certain way each time you start getting angry? (finding a common thread such as: isolating, drinking after, avoiding contact with loved ones, etc.)

What usually starts a fight, bout of anger, or outburst? (What seems to trigger you?)

What survival modes did you check off? How do these correlate with the emotions described alongside them?

Discovering different ways of reading your own body will not happen overnight. But this process is all about learning to trust yourself. Then, when you can see the common threads in your actions and reactions, understanding yourself and regaining control will soon follow.

23

FEEL-GOOD ACTIVITIES

"Mental health isn't built only in hard moments, but in everything you do daily to feel good." – Dr. Thema Bryant

Happiness is crucial to healing trauma, and fun is one of the keys to finding happiness. Your brain is amazing in how it has learned to protect you. However, it remembers the trauma you experienced as a child and is still living life under stress. Joy is the best remedy for stress and trauma.

Happiness can be a complex emotion to feel. You may not think that you deserve to be happy. Or when you do, you may find yourself panicking that things are going too well. Your trauma may begin to activate the part of your brain, afraid something bad is about to happen.

Subconsciously, you might be afraid of letting yourself find happiness. That is why prioritizing fun and learning to choose joy is so important in healing and moving forward. It's time to give yourself the right to experience pleasure and happiness.

How Does a Traumatic Childhood Affect Happiness?

We learn how to experience emotions and express ourselves in our developmental years. This means that if your childhood was filled with stress, tension, and trauma, happiness could be hard to learn later on. Children are very impressionable and vulnerable to their environments, which makes us believe that we simply cannot be happy. This is not true. You need to learn some new skills and integrate a little bit of positivity each day.

Childhood trauma and abuse effectively make the adult version of you have difficulty finding peace of mind. This is where the struggle to find happiness comes in. The backdrop of your life was filled with discontent, fear, and sadness. With those feelings taking up most of your developmental years, finding joy and positivity feels like an afterthought.

This is why feeling safe, at peace, and comfortable are the foundational emotions of happiness. Because when you exist through a lens of safety and protection, positivity can flow into your life much more.

What Makes You Happy?

Moving through and processing trauma is complex; there is no denying that. But that doesn't mean your healing journey must always be heavy. When you have decided to pursue recovering from your wounds, adding fun and lightness into your daily life is crucial.

But what makes us happy? The answer to that question depends on the individual. Happiness can be cultivated through certain situations, but what makes you joyful is specific to you. Feel free to answer the questions below to brainstorm things, experiences, and other emotions that bring you joy:

What comforts you?

_____

_____

What is one thing you do or experience daily that brings positive feelings and makes you feel good?

_____

_____

_____

What is something you crave and know will make you feel good?

_____

_____

When do you feel the safest?

In what situations do you feel the most at peace?

Fun and Free Activities to Increase Happiness

To cultivate more positive emotions, practice light, exciting, and joyful activities in your daily life. These activities don't need to be big, grand, or expensive; they just need to bring you peace and happiness. While this may sound simple, it can be easier said than done. So, if you find this difficult, just know that you are not alone and that recovery is not always linear.

I firmly believe that the best things in life are free, and finding joy can be easy! Below is a list of different feel-good activities you can pick from and practice. This list is here to get you started discovering what makes you happy, so feel free to add to the list anytime (Alford, 2013)!

- Make a thankfulness journal— In this journal, you can start listing out one thing you are grateful for each day! Then, when you are feeling down, you can read all the things you were thankful for in the past.

- Meditate— Morning meditation to start your day right and set intentions for joy is an excellent way of living to find happiness. At night meditation can be used to reflect on your day and recenter yourself.

- Take a picture when you see something pretty, or that brings you joy— A picture is worth a thousand words, and having reminders of joy on your phone to access anytime is an excellent way of keeping that positivity with you!

- Play your favorite song and sing in the shower.

- Read a book you loved from childhood— Let yourself find that escape in a whimsical world and feel the joy of something your inner child craves.

- Play a board game with friends or family.

- Practice small acts of random kindness— Sometimes, showing others compassion is an excellent way of helping yourself get in a better mood and share positivity!

- Let yourself take an afternoon cat nap.

- Go on a walk around the block.

- Listen to your favorite podcast while doing mundane tasks— This is a great way of integrating fun and entertainment into daily life.

- Paint something— Whether you're an "artist" or not, painting something is always fun. It could be a finger painting, a piece of paper, or even a rock! Whatever you want to decorate, let yourself express your creativity through color.

- Get your body moving— You could run, practice yoga, or go to the gym! Whatever you enjoy doing that gets your blood pumping will instantly boost your mood.

- Watch your favorite comfort movie or TV show.

- Watch the stars or the clouds— Sometimes, just looking at the sky and letting yourself fully relax can help you relax and find a sense of peace that nothing else can offer.

- Light a candle.

- Call an old friend.

- Take yourself on a solo date — Treat yourself like a date would! Have fun with it, pamper yourself, get dressed up, and do something to show yourself some compassion.

Let's move on to some questions and prompts that can help you discover what the best activities for joy may be for you:

What was one activity that let you escape negative emotions and situations as a child? This could be an activity that made you happy or simply distract you.

What is something you find yourself doing after a long week? Does this make you happy, or does it only push your emotions down?

What is one thing you look forward to each week?

Do you have any hobbies that genuinely make you happy? If not currently, did you have any in the past?

Do you have one friend who makes you feel good about yourself whenever you see them? If so, how can you get together with them more often?

How do you usually feel after a day of work? If you typically feel down, how do you tend to soothe yourself?

When you can understand why happiness can be a complicated emotion to cultivate, how your childhood affected that, and learn easy activities that you can use, integrating joy into your life will be much more natural!

So let yourself discover what you genuinely enjoy each day, week, or month. Find activities that make you feel like you've never been sad before and permit yourself to feel safe, comfortable, and relaxed.

24

BUILD TRUST

"Building trust means showing you're reliable, even when no one is watching." – Anonymous

Trust is fundamental to building and upholding healthy relationships in any area of life. It is a central piece in our relationships, both romantic and platonic. However, all trust was shattered in the people you loved and looked up to most when you experienced childhood trauma or abuse. You learned early on not to trust the people around you. So, learning how to build trust, later on, can be hard. But that doesn't mean it is impossible.

Trust issues are something that people with childhood trauma exhibit as extreme levels of independence, fear of getting too close to people, and the inability to be vulnerable. All these things stop you from trusting the people you can trust and having loving relationships with. When you are going through the process of healing, you must learn to trust the people around you in healthy and manageable ways.

What is Trust?

Trust plays a crucial role in every aspect of our lives. From business and work relations to healthcare, romantic relationships, and family life— Trust is vital to building a healthy relationship with the world around you. Trust isn't just a set of behaviors; it can be evidence of confidence and trustworthiness. There are a few things that psychotherapists like to describe the process of trust (Thagard, 2018):

- Behaving in specific ways to express the feeling and comfort of trust.

- A belief is the probability that someone you have a relationship with will act in certain ways.

- Trust is a feeling of comfort, confidence, and security with a partner you believe cares.

- It is an abstract mental attitude that the person you have a relationship with will be dependable.

- Trust is based upon emotional reactions and triggers.

Trust is triggered when someone is nice or charismatic to us. The trust itself is not what we see on the outside, the specific behaviors that tell us someone trusts. These actions are a mere reflection of the emotions that we experience internally.

The feeling of trust is not one single emotion we feel. Trust is based upon a series of positive emotions we experience through a connection with another person or ourselves. We cannot trust ourselves when we have a poor relationship with who we are. When we experience negative emotions of discomfort and sadness with someone, trust will have no foundation to be established.

Vulnerability and Trust

You may think, "Pretty easy"; I know how to integrate positive emotions into my life." But that's not all it takes to establish trust. Trust, positive associations, and vulnerability are the essential building blocks of trusting relationships. When you can't be vulnerable with your partner, you won't be able to trust yourself or the relationship.

When I set out to create a relationship of trust with myself and the people around me, I had to learn to accept not knowing and feeling vulnerable. There was no escaping it. My partner was uncomfortable with how I was reacting and responding to him.

He told me he didn't like it when I asked his opinion, then I declined and asked him again. It was uncomfortable for me to hear, so I had two choices. First, I could stop, not work on myself, and run away from vulnerability. Or I could embrace what he was saying and listen. I knew anger and negative reactions would only hurt me and our relationship, so I decided to listen. It was time for me to let myself be vulnerable and learn to be better.

Vulnerability means being completely upfront, open, and honest with someone or perhaps with yourself. It takes trust, and trust requires vulnerability. These two traits are intertwined and cannot fully exist without each other. You will need to learn to accept help and feedback from others, understanding that they want the best for you. It's time to allow yourself to be open and honest and to make deeper connections.

Here are some questions you can ask yourself as you learn to trust yourself and the people around you:

Do you have difficulty accepting outside help?

Why do you think this way?

What emotions do you feel when you realize you need help to achieve a goal?

Do you often allow yourself to accept help?

Do you feel it is a bad thing to need help?

How to Build (or Rebuild) Trust in your relationships

Learning to Trust Yourself – Childhood sexual abuse can make you feel like you can't trust your intuition. It can be hard to let yourself be vulnerable, spend time alone, or listen to your mind and body. Here are some ways you can work to build trust with yourself once again and regain confidence in yourself:

Spend intentional time with yourself - Sitting alone in your room watching a movie isn't the kind of alone time I'm talking about. When learning to trust yourself again, Happy, lasting relationships require a strong foundation of trust. Without this, everything will implode. Here are some

tips for how you can work to build (or re-build) trust in your relationships (Morse, 2022):

Openly communicate - As I have mentioned before, being open and
honest with your partner is crucial to building trust. This means you
need to practice openly communicating as a regular habit. You will
gain your partner's trust by letting them know how you feel and what
you are going through. Using eye contact and being honest about your
feelings in the moment of the situation (and not later) will all work
to open up your communication effectively. You can start building
trust mutually when you both put in this effort.

Learn to set healthy boundaries - This goes along with being open
with communication. Partners should be able to share their boundaries, comfort zones openly, and limits with one another. Even further, respecting each other's boundaries, you have communicated
about will be where the trust is built and seen. Your boundaries
may include physical and emotional limits, social needs, or breathing
room.

Give one another the benefit of the doubt - You won't ever be able to read
your partner's mind, no matter how close you are. This means it's time to
switch your mindset from always being worried and skeptical to trusting
them until they have proven themselves unworthy. If you have a concern
or worry about something, bring it up to them, but be sure to give them
the benefit of the doubt. This is another way of practicing healthy and
open communication. But you also need to be sure you fully listen to their

perspective and that they have a chance to express themselves without interruption.

Practice respect - One of the best ways to build trust with your partner is to invest in reassuring one another that you are both working towards mutual respect. If you care for one another, then respect should be something you want to pursue. Treat them well, show them actions of love and support, and let them know that you are always there and will respect their decisions.

Commit to the words you say - Words are an important part of building and rebuilding trust in a relationship. But the reality is that they don't mean much if your actions don't reflect the words you are saying. You need to show your partner that your words are promises and that you expect the same from them. Making promises and following through is one of the greatest ways of rebuilding trust in any relationship.

Consistent check-ins with your partner - Communication is not a one-time thing. You need to check in with your partner from time to time to ensure everything is going alright. You need to see that you are both on the same page about what is going on in the relationship. Allowing both parties to express joys and concerns at specific times openly will make this communication a habit that you can learn to integrate regularly.

When you make mistakes, make them learn lessons - Mistakes are un-avoidable. You might hurt one another; it's just up to you how you react and move forward. A lack of trust will stem from hurt feelings, lies, and deceit. So, let your actions speak louder than your words. When you hurt your partner or make a mistake, do your best to find a solution and apologize, but don't stop there. Make a visible effort to keep trying to improve yourself and keep your word, so the same mistake isn't repeated.

Building, or re-building, trust is one thing, but maintaining that trust is something that needs constant work and effort. Below are some actions you can learn to make habits to cultivate and maintain trust in your relationships:

Show daily care and consideration - Make an effort with your partner to show them that you care. If you already know how they receive love the best, use this to show them consideration. Your partner will begin to feel more valued and want to offer you the same kind of care.

Follow through - Keep your word if you promise date nights once each week. If you talk about saving for a vacation, follow through. When you keep up with your promises, you will be more trustworthy and show your partner that this is expected in the relationship. This means they will learn to do the same, effectively maintaining existing trust.

You must sit with your thoughts, show yourself love, listen to your emotions, and spend quality time alone. This might look like journaling, going on a walk, or even listening to music and sitting with the emotions that come up.

Practice making decisions - You may feel like you can't trust your gut feeling or that you can't make the right decisions when you make decisions. The only way for you to start trusting yourself and you decide to practice. This can start small, maybe by choosing where you and your friends go to lunch, and can evolve through time and practice.

Be kind to yourself - It might sound obvious, but sometimes we all need the reminder to be kind and gentle with ourselves. We are our harshest critics, which means it can be hard to see ways we can be nice to ourselves. This means allowing yourself to exist as you are, accepting and lovingly working on your flaws, and reassuring yourself that you are enough as you are!

Set reasonable goals, and attain them - When you set a goal for yourself, follow through, and reach that goal, you are telling your brain that you can trust your intentions. If you are looking for action steps you can take to rebuild trust in yourself, try simply setting daily or weekly goals that you can check off and complete with reasonable energy and time allowed for yourself. This will help you gain confidence and learn to trust yourself more.

Now that you have discovered the tools to build and maintain trust in your relationships and yourself, you might still find yourself looking for more and wanting to put all of the ideas in this workbook into action. The next and final chapter will be about setting goals and getting what you crave from the healing process.

25

SET HEALING GOALS

"Without purpose, pain goes in circles. With purpose, it becomes transformation." – Inspired by Viktor Frankl

Setting goals for your healing is essential to tracking your progress, having something to work for, and focusing your energy on the right actions. Your goals will be personal and need to feel relevant to what you want to accomplish.

It's time for you to take over the recovery process fully. You have so much knowledge about healing, so now you just need to put that knowledge to use. Goals will help you move to new levels of recovery and keep you on track with the healing process.

What are Goals, and Why Are Goals Important?

Goals work to give you a sense of direction in your journey. Without them, you may end up spinning your wheels and never gaining traction. Even having small goals to get you started is better than having none at all.

To set goals for yourself is to create a roadmap to your future. When you can see clearly where you are going, you will develop motivation, fuel, and excitement about moving forward - having milestones to look forward to works to help the state of your trauma.

Even the smallest of goals give you a sense of accomplishment. When you slowly integrate little steps, your big recovery goals will be on the way faster than you could have ever imagined!

Goals are not wishes. They are simple, tangible actions you put your time and energy into making happen. They don't need to be extravagant, and they don't need to amaze the people around them. They inspire you to keep going, help you focus your mind, and give you hope and confidence.

It is important to note that when you begin setting goals, the journey is just as important as hitting your milestones. Enjoy the path you have created, focus your mind each day on what you are accomplishing, and watch as your goals become your reality!

How to Set Healing Goals

When you have the tools to begin healing, all that's left is being intentional with the process and creating the right goals. To set specific goals for healing, there are some things you need to keep in mind:

1. Make them achievable and realistic.

It can be easy to let our imaginations get the best of us. While allowing yourself to dream is good, you must learn to keep your goals realistic. It is admirable to have big goals, but if they are too vague or hard to reach, you may not find the motivation to do so. This means that when setting goals, make them something you can easily measure. When you have a specific goal, a set of steps to follow, and you can reach it within a set period, you have an attainable goal! It will feel a lot less overwhelming to start and keep you motivated to keep you going.

2. Personalized

Your goals need to feel close to your heart because if you don't relate to the result, you will not have the inspiration to reach them. When you begin setting healing goals, don't set them for other people or based on others. You need to be sure you are listening to your specific needs and recovery desires you you can create successful goals.

3. Collaborate with the people around you.

Yes, your goals need to be personal. However, allowing the people around you to help support you in your journey is just as essential. Your goals will be even more effective if you work with a therapist, close family, or friend who can help you reach your aspirations. They can help you refine and develop your goals and keep you accountable through collaboration.

4. Make them flexible

Goals should be checked regularly and re-negotiated when needed. When you can follow your goals and allow space for flexibility, you can shift your actions based on your needs. Your goals are not set in stone forever, and letting them evolve as you do is the best way to ensure they suit you best.

My first goal was to be able to give a name to my emotions. I wanted to continue doing the grounding practice above throughout the day as often as needed. Then, recognizing my responsibility in discussions with my partner started to come more easily (not always, but it was a step forward). I began understanding the importance of not waiting to explode when expressing myself. Work still needs to be done every day, and there is still a long way to go, but it's much better than before. We even managed to discuss wills and what we would do after each other's death. However, not too much. He has a Cartesian mind. I have a problematic relationship with money, which is anxiety-provoking. I try to enter those conversations in small doses.

When trying to discover the goals you want to set, I recommend the below questions and prompts as a great starting place:

What is bothering me in my current life that has led me to want to heal the wounds of sexual abuse? (make a list)

What are the current problems?

What have I learned about myself since I started reading this book?

What surprised me the most?

What will be different when the effects of sexual abuse are less present in your life?

What do you plan to do once the problems of sexual abuse are less present?

What would be your healing goal? (list a behavior or concrete action)

What indicator would tell that your goal is achieved?

Name one of your best qualities.

Name three activities in which you feel you can do well.

Name an achievement for which you feel most proud.

Set a personal goal and describe your steps to achieve it.

Goal:

Steps:

Setting healing goals does not need to be daunting or overly complicated. You can start simply by changing every aspect of your morning or night routine. When you allow yourself to start small, altering simpler areas of your life, you can move on to bigger goals and watch your life transform.

26

THE 7-DAY CHALLENGE

If you've had an opportunity to read my book, I'd love to hear what you think about it. I wrote it so that other victims like myself could become aware of what is blocking them internally and preventing them from recovering from the aftermath of sexual abuse. For a better self-awareness experience, I suggest a 7-day challenge. This tool helped me, along with the many exchanges with other victims in the support group, which I share to demystify certain prejudices.

The downloadable Document

Use this link to download the Grounding Technique 7-day Challenge.

Or scan this QR-Code

You will find the benefits of feeling grounded and the ability for naming your needs, once the challenge is completed. Writing a review will provide me with valuable feedback and help me identify areas for improvement as well as what you appreciate. Additionally, it motivates me to continue writing and honing my craft. Thank you!

Please, use one of the provided links below.

USA

https://Amazon.com/review/create-review?&asin=B0C7WHGW2B

Or, login to your Amazon and select "My orders".

Thank you so much for your help!

27

CONCLUSION

You are a survivor. **Remember that.** It takes courage to pick up a book like this, but you have made it, and now it's your turn to take over the rest of the healing process. You have taken the steps needed to move forward with a firm foundation. This workbook is here for you to return to whenever you need it. These exercises and strategies are here for practice and use throughout the rest of your healing path and life!

We have gone over survival modes and how to understand the ways you learned to cope throughout the years. Then it was time to discover and dive deeper into emotions that trigger and affect them. But just knowing what you have been doing in the past wasn't enough, and you have been equipped with the tools to tell your story and gain closure through exercises and writing.

You have discovered how to shift your mindset from a victim to a survivor to a warrior because you deserve to be proud of your progress! But even more than that, we have covered the different emotions you have felt and will feel in the future. Because even if you understand you are a warrior, there will still be hard days. This simply means you need to allow yourself to feel the emotions that come with the healing journey.

Your tool belt is now full of feel-good activities to boat your mood and lighten yourself through such a complicated process. Then, we learned that building trust and setting goals are your final keys to recovery. Nothing is left to hold you back when you know who you are, that you are allowed to be vulnerable, and that you have places to go in the future.

Thank you so much for reading this book! I am so proud of you. I hope you feel confident enough to keep pushing, pursue recovery, and keep up the fantastic work! If you found this book's knowledge, skills, healing techniques, and tools helpful, please let me know by leaving a review on or on https://Amazon.com/review/create-review?&asin=B0BW21B9DD

Thank you!

28

REFERENCES

5 étapes clés pour sortir de la victimisation. Green Hypnose. (2021, January 4). Retrieved January 31, 2023, from

Ackerman, C. E. (2022, December 17). Writing therapy: How to write and journal therapeutically. PositivePsychology.com. Retrieved January 30, 2023, from

Alford, C. (2013, March 20). 30 absolutely free activities that can make you happy today. Lifehack. Retrieved February 2, 2023, from

Barnhill, J. W. (2023, January 31). Posttraumatic stress disorder (PTSD) - mental health disorders. Merck Manuals Consumer Version. Retrieved February 4, 2023, from

Consequences. INSPQ. (n.d.). Retrieved January 27, 2023, from

Hartney, E. (2022, November 14). How do you know if you were sexually abused? Verywell Mind. Retrieved January 27, 2023, from

Khan, M. (2023, January 31). Substance use disorders - mental health disorders. Merck Manuals Consumer Version. Retrieved February 4, 2023, from https://www.merckmanuals.com/en-ca/home/mental-health-diso rders/substance-related-disorders/substance-use-disorders

Mayo Foundation for Medical Education and Research. (2022, February 3). How to stop negative self-talk. Mayo Clinic. Retrieved January 29, 2023, from

Morse, E. (2022, April 18). How to build and maintain trust in a relationship . MasterClass. Retrieved February 3, 2023, from https://www.masterclass.com/articles/trust-in-a-relationship

Newmark, G. (n.d.). Critical emotional needs of children - newopp.org. Emotionally Healthy Child. Retrieved January 31, 2023, from

Oh, H. (2012, October 23). Silence is for victims: Why sexual assault survivors need to speak up. Daily Sundial. Retrieved January 30, 2023, from

Overview of writing therapy & how it helps physically & psychologically. The Human Condition. (2023, January 2). Retrieved January 30, 2023, from

Raypole, C. (2019, December 12). Emotional contagion: What it is and how to avoid it. Healthline. Retrieved January 27, 2023, from

Staff, C. G. R. C. (2021, January 4). Trauma and the brain: Signs you might be living in "Survival mode". CGRC. Retrieved January 27, 2023, from

Thagard, P. (2018, October 9). What is trust? Psychology Today. Retrieved February 3, 2023, from

U.S. Department of Health and Human Services, NIH. (2021, April 13). Why is there comorbidity between substance use disorders and mental illnesses? National Institutes of Health. Retrieved February 4, 2023, from
.